The World According
to Al Qaeda

To order additional copies, please contact us.
BookSurge, LLC
www.booksurge.com
1-866-308-6235
orders@booksurge.com

BRAD
K. BERNER

THE WORLD
ACCORDING TO
AL QAEDA

2005

The World According to Al Qaeda

TABLE OF CONTENTS

If you wish to conduct offensive war you must know the men employed by the enemy. Are they wise or stupid, clever or clumsy? Having assessed their qualities, you prepare appropriate measures.

Sun Tzu *The Art of War*

When people are entering upon a war they do things the wrong way round. Action comes first, and it is only when they have already suffered that they begin to think.

Thucydides

For Flora

ABU GHRAIB PRISON, IRAQ

By the grace of Allah, the Mujahideen of the Arabian Peninsula...were able to successfully kidnap an American of the Christian religion...And the Mujahideen in the Arabian Peninsula committed their legal right in treatment of the Americans as they had treated our brothers in Guantanamo and Abu Ghraib.

Al Qaeda Organization in the Arabian Peninsula, 13 June 2004

You who shirk jihad, how can you enjoy sitting idly while your brethren in Iraq suffer greatly under the oppression of Allah's enemies, while you are with you wives? How can you enjoy life and comfort while your noble sisters are being raped and their honor defiled in the Abu Ghraib prison?...I believe you saw those pictures that came out of the Abu Ghraib prison. These pictures [reflect the situation] of our brethren in the prisons of Israel, in America, and [in the prisons of] their collaborators in the region.

Abu Abd al-Rahman al-Athari Sultan ibn Bijad, 17 November 2004.

AFGHANISTAN—THE WAR AGAINST THE U.S.S.R. (1979-1989)

What I lived in two years there [Afghanistan], I could not have lived in a hundred years elsewhere...When the invasion of Afghanistan started, I was enraged and went there at once—I arrived within days, before the end of 1979. Yes, I fought there, but my fellow Muslims did much more than I. Many of them died and I am still alive...No, I was never afraid of death. As Muslims, we believe that when we die, we go to heaven. Before a battle, Allah sends us...tranquility...Personally neither I nor my brothers saw evidence of American help.

Osama bin Laden, 6 December 1993.

To counter these atheist Russians, the Saudis chose me as their representative in Afghanistan...I did not fight against the communist threat while forgetting the peril from the West.... For us, the idea was not to get involved more than necessary in the fight against the Russians, which was the business of the Americans, but rather to show our solidarity with our Muslim brothers. I discovered that it was not enough to fight in Afghanistan, but that we had to fight on all fronts against Communist or Western oppression. The urgent thing was Communism, but the next target was America...This is an open war up to the end, until victory.

Osama bin Laden, April 1995.

We were never at any time friends of the Americans [in Afghanistan]. We knew that the Americans supported the Jews in Palestine and that they were our enemies. Most of the weapons that came to Afghanistan were paid for by the Saudis on the orders of the Americans because Turki al-Faisal [head of Saudi external intelligence] and the CIA were working together.

Osama bin Laden, 6 December 1996.

Allah stood with the Muslims, the Afghani Mujahideen, and those who fought with them from other Muslim countries. We fought against the Russians and the Soviet Union until, not to say we defeated them, but Allah defeated them. They became nonexistent. There is a lesson to learn from this for he who wishes to learn...The Soviet Union entered in the last week of 1979, in December, and with Allah's help their flag was folded on December 25, a few years later, and thrown in the trash. There was nothing left to call the Soviet Union.

Osama bin Laden, 28 May 1998.

We believe that those who participated in the jihad in Afghanistan bear the greatest responsibility in this regard, because they realized that with insignificant capabilities, with a small number of RPG's, with a small number of antitank mines, with a small number of Kalashnikov rifles, they managed to crush the greatest empire [the U.S.S.R.] known to mankind. They crushed the greatest military machine. The so-called superpower vanished into thin air.

Osama bin Laden, 10 June 1999.

AFGHANISTAN—THE TALIBAN REGIME
(1995-2001)

The Afghan government has not asked us to leave the country. All gratitude to Allah, our relationship with our brother Mujahideen in Afghanistan is a deep and broad relationship where blood and sweat have mixed as have the links over long years of struggle against the Soviets. It is not a passing relationship, nor one based on personal interests. They are committed to support the religion approved by Allah, and that the country remains as the Muslims have known it, a strong fort for Islam, and its people are amongst the most protective of the religion approved by Allah, and the keenest to fulfill His laws and to establish an Islamic state.

Osama bin Laden, October/November 1996.

The emir of the faithful, Mullah Mohammed Omar, managed, by the grace of Allah, to save Islamic jihad in Afghanistan after great sacrifices by the Muslim people... America managed, through its agents, and especially some Arab countries and Pakistan, to perpetuate the division of the strongest Islamic people in this region, a people that were able to turn the Soviet Union into a myth...The Taliban state has been subjected to great pressure by Russia and its agents, with the support of the Communists and by America, through its agents in the Arab region and Pakistan, in order to silence me...The Commander of the Faithful [Mullah Omar] is the only legitimate ruler of the state of Afghanistan, where Allah, praise and glory be to Him, has guided the steps of Muslims so that an Islamic country can be ruled by Allah's Shari'a for the first time in tens of years.

Osama bin Laden, 22 December 1998.

We do not expect to be driven out of this land... Afghanistan, having raised the banner of Islam and started to seek to apply the Shari'a of Islam, by the grace of Allah, has become a target of the Crusader-Jewish alliance. We expect Afghanistan to be bombarded, even though the non-believers will say that they do so because of the presence of Osama... We expect attacks that will target Afghanistan as a Muslim nation, or rather the only state in this age which has started to apply Islam, and all Muslims should support it. It is a state of scholars. All Muslims should focus their efforts...in support of this state.

Osama bin Laden, 22 December 1998.

Any aggression by the United States today against Afghanistan would not be against Afghanistan in itself, but against the Afghanistan that hoists the banner of Islam in the Muslim world...our relationship with them [the Taliban] is very strong and deep. This is an ideological relationship, based on doctrine, and not on political or commercial positions... today, Afghanistan is the only country in the world that has Shari'a. Therefore, it is compulsory upon all the Muslims all over the world to help Afghanistan, and to immigrate to this land, because it is from this land that we will dispatch our armies to smash all infidels all over the world.

Osama bin Laden, 22 June 2000.

[Al Qaeda training camp, Afghanistan, late 1990s] It had people from all nationalities, who were getting training there, and each group stayed together, those who will have some work to do together later on. Each group was formed depending on the country they came from...[nationalities at the camp] Jordanians, Algerians, from Yemen, from Saudi Arabia, from Sweden, from Germany also, French also, Turks also, and Chechens also.

Ahmed Ressam, July 2001.

No. We cannot do that [give up Osama bin Laden]. If we did, it means we are not Muslims...that Islam is finished. If we were afraid of attack, we could have surrendered him the last time we were threatened and attacked. So America can hit us again, and this time we don't even have a friend.

Mullah Omar, 21 September 2001.

AFGHANISTAN—U.S. INVASION/WAR (OCTOBER 2001—NOW)

We now live under this Crusader bombardment that targets the entire nation. The Muslim community should know that we defend a just cause.

Sulaiman Abu Ghaith, 9 October 2001.

We also would like to declare our full support for this emirate and for the Muslim Afghan people in the face of this ferocious assault, offering all the material and moral resources that we have under the command of Mullah Muhammad Omar, commander of the faithful...This holds true regardless of the duration of the war. The issue at hand is the issue of an entire nation that opposes humiliation and subservience under the yoke of U.S. arrogance and Jewish persecution.

Sulaiman Abu Ghaith, 13 October 2001.

Undoubtedly you are closely watching with all interest and empathy the Crusade which is being led by the United States of America, with the full support of Britain and the European Christian states, and NATO and Russia, and the ex-Communist states and whoever agrees with them from the people of the creed of disbelief, and the apostates and the cowards amongst the Muslims—they are gathering their armies and campaigning as one party against the Islamic Emirate of Afghanistan, aiming to fulfill one thing, which they themselves have announced: the termination and destruction of the Islamic government of Afghanistan; and end what they call 'bases of terrorism.'

Mullah Omar, 2 November 2001.

The problems planted by the United States and its allies in our country will not take us far from the Palestinian issue and the sacred mosque...and our American and Jewish enemies will be the losers at the end of this war.

Mullah Omar, 12 April 2002.

The deception episode continued to unfold as the United States entered into a direct war with the Mujahideen in Afghanistan [in October 2001] and tried to present itself to the world as a winner. It was a farcical performance featuring paper tigers as the main characters. All [U.S.] actions were portrayed as 'eliminating the last remnant of Al Qaeda and the Taliban,' 'carrying out the last operation,' 'destroying the last cave,' and 'controlling the last position.' So much so that the 'last' became endless.

Al-Ansar, 12 June 2002.

I am happy to tell you that the jihad in Afghanistan is going well...and that things are improving in favor of the Mujahideen, thanks to Allah. We are now in the second year of fighting, and America has not managed to accomplish its objectives; on the contrary, it has become embroiled in the Afghan swamp...the Afghans have relied—after placing their trust in Allah—on their [greatest] strength, namely, their ability to conduct guerrilla warfare from the depths of their impassable mountains, using the same tactics with which, thanks to Allah, they had previously defeated the Soviet army...America's defeat in Afghanistan will be, Allah willing, the beginning of its end.

Osama bin Laden, 11 February 2003.

[President Hamid] Karzai is a collaborator who was brought in by the Americans, and so to support him against the Muslims is one of the ten acts which violate Islam and exclude the perpetrator from the Muslim community.

Osama bin Laden, 11 February 2003.

All the efforts the American enemy exerted confirm their bad intentions to establish a double agent leadership, and divide the country and steal its wealth. Therefore, America cannot change the Afghani view about it. Currently, the imposed government in Kabul does not control anything but the palace it lives in, and the coalition forces now are creating excuses to leave Afghanistan. But the Mujahideen are still in the battlefield, and the fight continues and will not end, Allah willing, until Afghanistan returns to Shari'a and Islam once more.

Saif al-Adel, March 2003.

Two years after Tora Bora [battle, December 2001], we are still, as we had been, with the blessings of Allah, pursuing the Americans and their allies everywhere and, in fact, in their own backyard…the American collapse in Afghanistan has become an explicit reality.

Ayman al-Zawahiri, 19 December 2003.

AIDS

You [the United States] have been described in history as a nation that spreads diseases that were unknown to man in the past. Go ahead and boast to the nations of man that you brought them AIDS as a Satanic American Invention.

Al Qaeda, 24 November 2002.

AL QAEDA

Every principle needs a vanguard to carry it forward and, while focusing its way into society, puts up with heavy tasks and enormous sacrifices. There is no ideology, neither earthly nor heavenly, that does not require such a vanguard that gives everything it possesses in order to achieve victory for this ideology. It carries the flag all along the sheer, endless and difficult path until it reaches its destination in the reality of life, since Allah has destined that it should make it and manifest itself. This vanguard constitutes *al-Qa'idah al-Sulbah* for the expected society.

Abdullah Azzam, April 1988.

[Al Qaeda's role is] to instigate the Muslim community to get up and liberate its land, to fight for the sake of Allah, and to make Shari'a the highest law, and the word of Allah the highest word of all.

Osama bin Laden, 10 June 1999.

I must say that my duty is just to awaken the Muslims...Al Qaeda was set up to wage a jihad against infidelity, particularly to counter the onslaught of the infidel countries against the Islamic states.

Osama bin Laden, 28 September 2001.

The name "Al Qaeda" was established a long time ago by mere chance. The late Abu Ubaida al-Banshiri [Al Qaeda military commander, d. 1996] established the training camps for our Mujahideen against Russia's terrorism. We used to call the training camp Al Qaeda ["the base"], and the name stayed. We speak about the conscience of the Muslim community; we are the sons of the Muslim community. We are brothers in Islam from the Middle East, Philippines, Malaysia, India, Pakistan, and as far as Mauritania.

Osama bin Laden, 21 October 2001.

The [premises] on which we base ourselves as an organization, and on which we base our operations and our method of action, are practical and realistic...They are also scientific and [in accordance with] Shari'a, and they give us confidence and certainty.

Sulaiman Abu Ghaith, 12 June 2002.

Our Muslim community is rich with many resources and capabilities, and the absolutely most important is the Muslim person who is the battle's fuel and the conflict's motor...If the particular groups [like Al Qaeda] have their role that others do not [incitement], then the general groups are the real fuel of the battle and the explosive material. The role of the particular groups is that of the detonator and the motor that detonates the material.

Osama bin Laden, 14 October 2002.

To clarify a very important basic principle: Al Qaeda is not fighting in the name of [or: in the place of] the Muslim community. On the contrary, it constitutes a blessed vanguard of [or: on behalf of] that Muslim community, which guides the way [for it], and illuminates it and [even] leads the Muslim community in striking out at its foe.

Salim al-Makhi, "The Master Trap." October/November 2002.

The American assault on Al Qaeda in Afghanistan has significantly 'raised the level of the organization.' Because its prominent dimensions in Afghanistan have disappeared, and rather than settle in a known place, it has become a complex secret program and an enterprise of martyrdom spread out all over the world. Therefore, the annihilation of Al Qaeda has become an impossible mission, and [for this reason] the American administration will reap the [seeds] of its foolish deeds.

Salim al-Makhi, "Mending the Hearts of the Believers." October/November 2002.

America today is facing a huge problem with Clausewitz's theories. The latter are premised on the existence of a centralized hostile power with a unified command. Assuredly, the Mujahideen, with the Al Qaeda organization in their vanguard, believe in decentralized organizations. Thus the enemy cannot ascertain the [Mujahideen] center of gravity, let alone aim a mortal blow at it.

Abu Ubayd al-Qurashi, 19 December 2002.

The organization of the jihadi base, known as Al Qaeda, is the organization of the Muslim community, and it is based on its creed and defends its interests. The members of Al Qaeda are the sons of the Muslim community whose faith is Islam. All the [financial] and material capabilities of Al Qaeda are the sum of the 'savings' of the Muslim community used to seek Allah's blessing, be He praised.

Saif al-Adel, March 2003.

It [Al Qaeda] is the vanguard of the Muslim community that has decided to fight you [the United States] to the last breath.

Ayman al-Zawahiri, 10 September 2003.

The problem is that today Al Qaeda is not an organization in the true sense of the word but only an idea that has become a faith...Many among the youth have begun to believe in Al Qaeda's views and beliefs regarding the struggle against America.

Nasser Ahmad Nasser al-Bahri, 3 August 2004.

AL QAEDA IN IRAQ

A large number of Al Qaeda operatives have entered Iraq, and they are currently fighting in the ranks of the Iraqi resistance...Abu Mus'ab al-Zarqawi was in Afghanistan and in Kabul. He met with Osama bin Laden a great many times, but I do not believe that he is number one in the Al Qaeda organization, since Al Qaeda has Iraqi leaders present on the ground in Iraq, and they are not in need of al-Zarqawi.

Nasser Ahmad Nasser al-Bahri, 3 August 2004.

The jihad fighters in Iraq have already taught us to oppose patriotism, national identity and regional particularism. They have set their sights on the collaborating government brought by the occupation, and they have shown us that which has brought pleasure to the believers [i.e. attacks]...O sheikh of the slaughterers, Abu Mus'ab [al-Zarqawi], go forth in the straight path with Allah's help, guided by Allah, fight together with the monotheists against the idol-worshippers, together with the warriors of jihad against the collaborators, the hypocrites and the rebellious.

Abd al-Rahman ibn Salem al-Shamari, August/September 2004.

We announce that al-Tawhid wa al-Jihad, its emir [Abu Mus'ab al-Zarqawi] and soldiers have pledged allegiance to the Mujahideen Osama bin Laden...Our brothers in Al Qaeda understood the strategy of Al-Tawhid wal Jihad group in the Land of the Two Rivers and were satisfied with our line.

Tawhid and Jihad, 17 October 2004.

[The Al Qaeda Organization in Iraq] has set for itself a number of central goals which are mutually interrelated and complementary:

- Renewing pure monotheism which was brought by our Prophet Muhammad...

- Jihad for the sake of Allah, so that His messenger be supreme, and in order to recapture all the lands of the Muslims from the hands of the infidels and the apostates, and to apply the Shari'a law...

- To come to the aid of Muslims wherever they are and to reclaim the Muslim's dignity, which has been soiled by the [foreign] invaders and their agents, and his human rights of which he has been deprived...

- To re-establish the Rightly-Guided Caliphate in accordance with the Prophet's example...

- The return of the Caliphate to Baghdad...

- The killing of al those fighting in the ranks of the infidel ('the police and the intelligence agents and all those that aid the Americans')

This is not an issue of Iraq in the geographic sense; rather it is an issue for our great Islam. Don't you see how all the infidels in the world have united and assembled armies from more than 30 countries to invade Iraq, to plunder its resources, to humiliate you and to violate your wives' honor. So why should your brothers, the jihad fighters—both foreigner and native—be subject to reproach? These brothers of yours emigrated from their homelands, left their wives and children, and sacrificed their blood for your sake—to protect you, to protect your families, and to preserve your honor, and to drive the invaders from your land.

Abu Maysara, 2 March 2005.

Every time the infidels loose a battle and suffer a humiliating defeat at the hands of the Mujahideen, they turn around and say they are winning the war against the so-called "resistance."

Al Qaeda in Iraq, 4 April 2005.

We, the Al Qaeda Organization in the Land of the Two Rivers, further announce to the entire world that, whoever joins the ranks of the cross worshippers, Jews, and apostates, should expect one verdict and one verdict only...We warn anyone who is thinking about joining the political process of the infidels and apostates that we will come to him with the sharp sword.

Al Qaeda in Iraq, 24 April 2005.

Here we are; two years have passed since Baghdad fell to the Crusaders. The Crusaders harvested nothing but defeat, shame and humiliation. Allah's grace and guidance (bestowed on the Mujahideen) have prevented the cross worshippers from realizing any of their goals for which they invaded Iraq. They envisioned taking control of this Muslim community, thereby paving the way for establishing the long sought after Zionist state from the Nile to the Euphrates.

Abu Mus'ab al-Zarqawi, 29 April 2005.

It is now becoming noticed that the Jews and the Crusaders are resorting to devious methods and despicable ways and means to harm the Mujahideen every time the intensity of attacks against them increases. They do so in order to suppress the stream of current attacks against them. They are often seen detaining women in order to put pressure on their relatives to stop jihad. They besiege cities and cut off their sources of the means of living. They destroy the infrastructure and the basic water and power lines and other public services, after which they conduct a campaign of breaches and searches in the homes of people, resulting in packed prisons with young and old men and even children.

Al Qaeda in Iraq, 14 May 2005.

ALGERIA

When the Islamic party [Islamic Salvation Front] in Algeria wanted to practice democracy and they won the election [1992], you [the United States] unleashed your agents in the Algerian army onto them to attack them with tanks and guns, and to imprison them and torture them—a new lesson from the 'American book of democracy'!!!

Al Qaeda, 24 November 2002.

We strongly and fully support Osama bin Laden's jihad against the heretic America as well as we support our brothers in Afghanistan, the Philippines and Chechnya.

Salafist Group for Preaching and Combat, September 2003.

Our connection to Al Qaeda and the other Jihad organizations in the world is based on two things: First, the operation of the Salafist Group for Preaching and Combat... is an operation integrated with that of the other groups, because [the Group] is a phased means aimed ultimately at establishing a group of Muslims—the Caliphate—and it sees this as a sacred goal that all Muslims must strive to attain... Second, one of our goals is also to educate the Muslims about the principle of loyalty to Islam...The Muslim is the brother of the Muslim, even if their countries are distant from each other. Every Muslim is entitled to the support [of other Muslims]... We support those who support Allah, His Prophet, and the believers, and we act with hostility towards those who act with hostility towards Allah and His Prophet, even if he is from among the closest of the close.

Nabil Sahraoui, 9 January 2004.

Don't forget your brothers in Algeria who have been fighting for Allah for more than ten years. [These fighters] have suffered from the abandonment of those close to them, from the enmity of those far from them, from the enemy's assault, and from afflictions and tribulations, but this has not weakened them. We appreciate them, and Allah will grant them their reward. We ask Allah to grant victory to them and to the other jihad fighters everywhere.

Sa'ud bin Hamoud al-Utaybi, October 2004.

[Despite demoralization] jihad in Algeria is ready...we are targeting the Jews and Crusaders, individuals, embassies, and interests that are the enemy's...The Muslim community is united in attacking them everywhere.

Abu Soheib Miliani, 8 May 2005.

ALLIES OF THE U.S.

What do your governments want by allying themselves with the criminal gang in the White House against Muslims? Do your governments not know that the White House gangsters are the biggest butchers of this age?...What do your governments want from their alliance with America in attacking us in Afghanistan? I mention in particular Britain, France, Italy, Canada, Germany and Australia.

Osama bin Laden, 12 November 2002.

We reserve the right to retaliate at the appropriate time and place against all countries involved [in the Iraq war], especially the UK, Spain, Australia, Poland, Japan and Italy, not to exclude those Muslim states that took part, especially the Gulf States, and in particular Kuwait, which has become a launch pad for the crusading forces.

Osama bin Laden, 18 October 2003.

AMERICAN PEOPLE

[The American people] are not exonerated from responsibility, because they chose this government and voted for it despite their knowledge of its crimes in Palestine, Lebanon, Iraq and in other places, and its support of its agent regimes that filled our prisons with our best children and scholars.

Osama bin Laden, March 1997.

Islamic religious scholars have issued a fatwa against any American who pays taxes to his government. He has become our target because he is providing assistance to the American war machine against the Muslim community.

Osama bin Laden, 22 December 1998.

You may have heard these days that almost three-quarters of the U.S. people support Clinton's strikes on Iraq. They are a people whose president becomes more popular when he kills innocent people. They are a people who increase their support for their president when he commits some of the seven cardinal sins. They are a lowly people who do not understand the meaning of principles.

Osama bin Laden, 10 June 1999.

Those who have experienced pleasure will not have the strength of character to withstand a long world war...The infidels will not be able to bear a life of terror with the sword of Damocles hanging over them.

Abu-Yasir Rifa'i Ahmad Taha, 12 November 2000.

When the sword comes down [on America], after 80 years, hypocrisy rears its ugly head. They deplore and they lament for those killers who have abused the blood, honor and sanctuaries of Muslims. The least that can be said about those people is that they are debauched. They have followed injustice. They supported the butcher over the victim, the oppressor over the innocent child. May Allah show them His wrath and give them what they deserve.

Osama bin Laden, 7 October 2001.

Allah, may He be glorified, outlines in this passage [on the supporters of the Crusaders] three matters:

1. The forbiddance of allying with the Jews and Christians and supporting them.

2. That whoever supports them, and helps them then the ruling upon him is the same as the ruling upon them.

3. That supporting them is from the character and signs of the hypocrites.

Mullah Omar, 2 November 2001.

The American people should remember that they pay taxes to their government, they elect their president, their government manufactures arms and gives them to Israel, and Israel uses them to massacre Palestinians. The America Congress endorses all government measures, and this proves that the entire America is responsible for the atrocities perpetrated against Muslims.

Osama bin Laden, 7 November 2001.

It is a fundamental principle of any democracy that the people choose their leaders and, as such, they approve and are party to the actions of their elected leaders...By electing these leaders, the American people have given their consent to the incarceration of the Palestinian people, the demolition of Palestinian homes, and the slaughter of the children of Iraq. This is why the American people are not innocent. The American people are active members in all these crimes.

Osama bin Laden, 14 October 2002.

As to the Americans...or if you prefer, say: scum...a nation of debaucherers...rootless [or: without lineage]...[a nation of] highway robbers...thieves...criminals...butchers of the Indians...slaves of the Jews...stray dogs and pigs for hire...for two hundred years, during which they shed the blood of over 4 million Muslims...[and also] the blood of scores of millions of people.

Salim al-Makhi, "The Master Trap." October/November 2002.

The American people are the ones who choose their government by way of their own free will; a choice which stems from their agreement with its policies. Thus the American people have chosen, consented to, and affirmed their support for the Israeli oppression of the Palestinians...The American people are the ones who pay the taxes which fund the planes that bomb us in Afghanistan, the tanks that strike and destroy our homes in Palestine, the armies which occupy our lands in the Arabian Gulf, and the fleets which ensure the blockade of Iraq...This is why the American people cannot be innocent of all the crimes committed by the Americans and Jews against us.

Al Qaeda, 24 November 2002.

It is saddening to tell you that you are the worst civilization witnessed by the history of mankind. You separate religion from your policies...

You are the nation that permits usury, which has been forbidden by all the religions. Yet you build your economy and investments on usury. As a result of this, in all its different forms and guises, the Jews have taken control of your economy, through which they have then taken control of your media, and now control all aspects of your life, making you their servants and achieving their aims at your expense...

You are a nation that permits acts of immorality, and you consider them to be pillars of personal freedom...You are a nation that permits gambling in all its forms. The companies practice this as well, resulting in the investments becoming active and the criminals becoming rich...

Your law is the law of the rich and wealthy people, who hold sway in their political parties and fund their election campaigns with their gifts. Behind them stand the Jews, who control your policies, media and economy.

Al Qaeda, 24 November 2002.

Some have the impression that you are a reasonable people. But the majority of you are vulgar and without sound ethics or good manners. You elect the evil from among you, the greatest liars and the least decent, and you are enslaved by your richest and the most influential among you, especially the Jews, who lead you using the lie of democracy to support the Israelis and their schemes, and in complete antagonism towards our religion [Islam].

Osama bin Laden, 18 October 2003.

The world considers the American people to be an uncivilized and barbaric nation that does nothing but appreciate aggression against others, only killing and a lust for bloodshed...The killing and torturing and attacking and even the way they speak with other people; their eating and drinking habits and the way they walk and the way they refuse to respect the law—all these images have made the Muslims more certain about the savageness of this nation...The American people are an ignorant people. It is even the most ignorant nation in the world and [its government] can easily manipulate the minds of its citizens.

The Islamic Army in Iraq, 2 January 2004.

AMERICAN PEOPLE, AL QAEDA TO THE

We tell the Americans as a people, and we tell the mothers of soldiers, and American mothers in general, if they value their lives and those of their children, find a nationalistic government that will look after their interests and not the interests of the Jews.

Osama bin Laden, 28 May 1998.

I ask the American people to force their government to give up anti-Muslim policies. The American people rose against their government's war in Vietnam. They must do the same today. The American people should stop the massacre of Muslims by their government.

Osama bin Laden, 7 November 2001.

By means of this document we send a message to America and those behind it. We are coming, by the will of Allah Almighty. No matter what America does, it will never be safe from the fury of Muslims. America is the one who began the war, and it will lose the battle by the permission of Allah Almighty.

Al Qaeda, 24 April 2002.

A message to the American people: Peace be upon those who follow the right path. I am an honest adviser to you. I urge you to seek the joy of life and the afterlife, and to rid yourselves of your dry, miserable, and spiritless materialistic existence. I urge you to become Muslims, for Islam calls for the principle of "There is no God but Allah," for justice, and forbids injustice and criminality. I call on you to understand the lesson of the New York and Washington raids [11 September 2001], which came in response to some of your previous crimes. The aggressor deserves punishment.

Osama bin Laden, 26 October 2002.

What do we want from you? The first thing that we are calling you to is Islam...The second thing well call you to, is to stop your oppression, lies, immorality and debauchery that has spread among you...

What we call you to thirdly is to take an honest stance with yourselves—and I doubt you will do so—to discover that you are a nation without principles or manners, and that values and principles to you are something which you merely demand from others, not that which you yourselves must adhere to.

We also advise you to stop supporting Israel, and to end your support of the Indians in Kashmir, the Russians against the Chechens, and to also cease supporting the Manila government against the Muslims in the southern Philippines.

We also advise you to pack your luggage and get out of our lands. We desire for you goodness, guidance and righteousness, so do not force us to send you back as cargo in coffins.

Sixthly, we call upon you to end your support of the corrupt leaders in our countries. Do not interfere in our politics and method of education. Leave us alone, or else expect us in New York and Washington.

We also call you to deal with us and interact with us on the basis of mutual interests and benefits, rather than the policies of sub dual, theft and occupation, not to continue your policy of supporting the Jews because this will result in more disasters for you.

If you fail to respond to these conditions, then prepare to fight the Muslim community... the community that rejects your attacks, wishes to remove your evils, and is prepared to fight you. You are well aware that the Muslim community, from the very core of its soul, despises your haughtiness and arrogance.

If the Americans refuse to listen to our advice and the goodness, guidance and righteousness that we call them to, then be aware that you will lose this Crusade Bush began, just like the other previous Crusades in which you were humiliated by the hands of the Mujahideen, fleeing to your home in great silence and disgrace. If the Americans do not respond, then their fate will be that of the Soviets who fled from Afghanistan to deal with their military defeat, political break up, ideological downfall and economic bankruptcy.

Al Qaeda, 24 November 2002.

Oh American people, you are the victim of your leaders, but you are also a partner in the war on us, because you applauded them when they killed the children of Iraq; applauded the Jews when they killed the children of Palestine...Allah has cursed you in this world and in the Hereafter and promised you terrible tortures. Defiantly, you have not learned your lesson from which you suffered: the raids on Washington and New York.

Abu Shihad al-Qandahari, 1 December 2002.

Bush has sent your sons into the lion's den [Iraq], to slaughter and be slaughtered, claiming that this act was in defense of international peace and America's security, thus concealing the facts.

Osama bin Laden, 18 October 2003.

I say to the American people, we will continue to fight you and continue to conduct martyrdom operations inside and outside the United States until you depart from your oppressive course and abandon your follics and rein in your fools...we will fight you as long as we carry our guns. And if we fall, our sons will take our place. And may our mothers become childless if we leave any of you alive on our soil.

Osama bin Laden, 18 October 2003.

My fellow countrymen, you are guilty, guilty, guilty, guilty. You are as guilty as Bush and Cheney. You're as guilty as Rumsfeld and Ashcroft and Powell. After decades of American tyranny and oppression, now it's your turn to die. Allah willing, the streets of America will run red with blood, matching drop for drop the blood of America's victims...the magnitude and ferocity of what is coming your way will make you forget all about September 11.

Assam the American, 28 October 2004.

Contrary to Bush's claim that we hate freedom, let him explain why we did not attack Sweden, for example. Clearly, those who hate freedom—unlike the 19 [11 September 2001 hijackers], may Allah have mercy on them—have no self-esteem. We have been fighting you because we are free men who do not remain silent in the face of injustice. We want to restore our Muslim community's freedom. Just as you violate our security, we violate yours. Whoever toys with the security of others, deluding himself that he will remain secure, is nothing but a foolish thief. One of the most important things rational people do when calamities occur is to look for their causes so as to avoid them...Your security is not in the hands of Kerry, or Bush or Al Qaeda. Your security is in your own hands, and any [U.S.] state that does not toy with our security automatically guarantees its own security.

Osama bin Laden, 29 October 2004.

I say to Americans, vote for whomever you want: Bush or Kerry, or even the devil—it is not of any importance...What concerns us is to purify our nation from the aggressors and to resist whoever [is] attacking us, profaning our sanctities and stealing our wealth.

Ayman al-Zawahiri, 29 November 2004.

ARAB REGIMES

As for the regimes, it has been proven beyond any doubt that they are useless and don't care for anybody. Under these circumstances, Muslims should carry out their obligations, since the rulers of the region have accepted the invasion of their countries. But these countries belong to Islam and not to those rulers. May Allah exact his revenge against all of them.

Osama bin Laden, 22 December 1998.

Allah's curse be upon the non-believing leaders and all the apostate Arab rulers who torture, kill, imprison and torment Muslims.

Al Qaeda, 10 May 2000.

Those who appointed [President Hamid] Karzai of Kabul [Afghanistan] and shaped 'Karzai' of Pakistan appointed 'Karzai' of Kuwait, 'Karzai' of Bahrain, 'Karzai' of Qatar and the other states. Those who appointed 'Karzai' of Riyadh one hundred years ago and brought him in, after he had been a refugee in Kuwait, to fight alongside them against the Ottoman state... were the Crusaders. They still protect this family [Saudi royal family]. There is no difference between the 'Karzai' of Riyadh and the Karzai of Kabul...these rulers have betrayed Allah and his Prophet, and they have expelled themselves from the Muslim community and betrayed the Muslim community.

Osama bin Laden, 11 February 2003.

The rulers of the Muslim community, without exception, are useless to their faith and their Muslim community, and they are no longer useful to the authority that appointed them.

Saif al-Adel, March 2003.

The shameful fact that we must not overlook is that all the countries of the Gulf Cooperation Council are occupied. The occupation took place without losses in the ranks of the enemy because it was an unconditional, complete surrender. Kuwait became an American base without any fighting. In the Land of the Two Holy Mosques there are military settlements that have surrounded Mecca and Medina without any fighting. Therefore, the foreign occupation exists throughout the region.

Al-Ansar, 17 April 2003.

The region's rulers deceive us and support infidels, and then claim they still cling to Islam.

Osama bin Laden, July 2003.

But the question strongly raised is: Are the governments in the Islamic world capable of pursuing their duty to defend the faith and the Muslim community, and renouncing all allegiance to the United States?...The Gulf States proved their total inability to resist the Iraqi forces [in 1990-1]. They sought help from the Crusaders, led by the United States. These states then came to America's help and backed it in its attack against an Arab state [Iraq in 2003].

Osama bin Laden, 4 January 2004.

ASSASSINATIONS

Other missions [of the Military Organization] consist of the following: ...Assassinating enemy personnel as well as foreign tourists...

Importance of the Military Organization: Removal of those personalities that block the call's path. All types of military and civilian intellectuals and thinkers for the state.

Al Qaeda, 10 May 2000.

An example of a Security Plan for a Group Mission (assassinating an important person): Assassination is an operation of military means and basic security. Therefore, it is essential that the commanders who establish plans related to assassination give attention to two issues:

First issue: The importance of establishing a careful, systematic, and solid security plan to hide the operation from the enemy until the time of its execution...

Second issue: The importance of establishing a tactical plan for the assassination operation that consists of the operational factors themselves (members, weapons, hiding places...) and factors of the operation (time, place)...

Al Qaeda, 10 May 2000.

A person, for example, that you plan to assassinate, you would first observe him, surveil him. You watch when he comes in and leaves, and you find where he lives, and you find out where his vulnerabilities are, and that is the place where you pick.

Ahmed Ressam, July 2001.

As for Arab nations, operations should expand to include the assassination of influential and effective personalities.

Manual of Afghan Jihad, 2 February 2002.

We have to target Jews and Christians. We have to let anybody that fights Allah, His Prophet or the believers know that we will be killing them. There should be no limits and no geographical borders. We have to turn the land of the infidels into hell as they have done to the land of the Muslims...The primary targets should be Jews and Christians who have important status in the Islamic countries. The purpose is not to allow them to settle in the lands of the Muslims. Our advice is to start with unprotected soft targets and the individuals from countries that support the local renegades.

For example, in the Holy Land [Saudi Arabia], the primary target should be Americans, then the British. In Iraq, the Americans first, in Afghanistan, the Americans first, and in Algiers, the French, and in Indonesia the Australians and so on.

The importance of the targets should be as follows:
1. Jews: They are at different levels. American and Israeli Jews first, the British Jews and then French Jews and so on.
2. Christians: Their importance is as follows: Americans, British, Spanish, Australians, Canadians and Italians

Abdul Aziz al-Muqrin, 29 March 2004.

America has offered great rewards to those who kill the militants fighting for Allah, and we in the Al Qaeda network are committed, Allah willing, to bestowing a prize of ten thousand grams of gold to anyone who kills the occupier Bremer [Paul Bremer, U.S. administrator in Iraq], his deputy, the American

Forces Commander or his deputy in Iraq...whoever kills Kofi Anan [Secretary General of the U.N.] or the president of the U.N. mission in Iraq or its representatives...will be given a prize of then thousand grams of gold.

Osama bin Laden, 6 May 2004.

Our Mujahideen within the framework of the Operation Retribution successfully carried out the special operation [assassination of Chechen President Akhmad Kadyrov on 9 May]...The Chechen people celebrated a double holiday on 9 May—the victory over Fascism and a small but very important victory over Russianism.

Shamil Basayev, 17 May 2004.

If two apostate authors are simultaneously liquidated in two different countries, it will require the security for thousands of writers in the Islamic world.

Abu Bakr Naji, 2 March 2005.

AUSTRALIA

I met Hambali [Indonesian Jemaah Islamiyah operative and Al Qaeda link], and we discussed about the possibility to do something in Sydney, during the Olympic Games there, this year [2000]. I discussed with him [Al Qaeda operative Mukhtar] about doing something in Australia...looking for a target in Australia which if it happens will result in a heavy impact on the Jews in Australia. The main objective here is that this operation will not only be done once...in the future we will do something again and disappear.

Jack Roche, 2002.

We warned Australia before not to join in [the war] in Afghanistan, and [against] its despicable effort to separate East Timor. It ignored the warning until it woke up to the sounds of explosions in Bali [12 October 2002]. Its government falsely claimed that they [the Australians] were not targeted.

Osama bin Laden, 12 November 2002.

We decided to settle accounts with Australia, one of the worst enemies of Allah and Islam...and a Mujahideen brother succeeded in carrying out a martyr operation with a car bomb against the Australian embassy. We advise all Australians in Indonesia to leave, or we will make it a grave for them, Allah willing...In the case the government does not comply with our demands, we will direct numerous painful blows, Allah willing, against them and the queue of car bombs will not stop.

Jemaah Islamiyah, 9 September 2004.

BALI, INDONESIA, BOMBINGS (12 OCTOBER 2002)

The Bali bombing was the response of a small group of Muslims who truly understand what it means to defend the dignity of Islam...We target the invaders...We target evil, arrogant nations proud of the destruction they have caused—with no country able to stop them...The Bali bombings were from a resistance to the American colonizers and its allies... Attacking civilians from the colonizer countries is reasonable and undertaken in the interests of balance and justice. Blood is repaid by blood, life by life, civilian by civilian.

Imam Samudra, September 2004.

BEHEADINGS

How can a free Muslim sleep soundly while Islam is being slaughtered, its honor bleeding and the images of shame in the news of the Satanic abuse of the Muslim men and women in the prison of Abu Ghraib...we offered the American administration the chance to exchange this prisoner [Nicholas Berg] for some of the prisoners at Abu Ghraib, but they refused. We say to you, the dignity of the Muslim men and women in the prison of Abu Ghraib and others will be redeemed by blood and souls. You will see nothing from us except corpse after corpse and casket after casket of those slaughtered in this fashion.

Abu Mus'ab al-Zarqawi, 11 May 2004.

[Khobar, Saudi Arabia, 29 May 2004] We found a Swedish infidel. Brother Nimr cut off his head, and put it at the gate [of the building] so that it would be seen by all those entering and exiting. We continued in the search for the infidels, and we slit the throats of those we found among them...We began to comb the site looking for infidels. We found Filipino Christians. We cut their throats and dedicated them to our brothers, the Mujahideen in the Philippines. We found Hindu engineers, and we cut their throats, too. Afterwards, we turned to the hotel. We entered and found a restaurant, where we ate breakfast and rested a while. Then we went up to the next floor, found several Hindu dogs, and cut their throats.

Fawwaz bin Muhammad al-Nashami, June 2004.

The Mujahideen did the execution [beheading] of the American prisoner [Paul Johnson] after the end of the interval period which the Mujahideen specified to the tyrants of the Saudi government, and this despicable person will receive his portion of justice in the other life hereafter, and let him taste something of what the Muslims have tasted who have likewise suffered under the American Apache aircraft [which he maintained] from their fire and suffering from their bullets and rockets...And to the Americans and their loyal allies from the world of heresy and criminality who are allied in their war against Islam, verily this action is a punishment to them.

Al Qaeda Organization in the Arabian Peninsula, 19 June 2004.

THE WORLD ACCORDING TO AL QAEDA

Our message is to you, the government of [South] Korea
and the Korean people: we call you to withdraw your forces
from our land and not send new additional troops to this land
[Iraq]. Otherwise, we will send you the head of this Korean
[Kim Sun-il] and heads of your other soldiers will follow.

Jammat al-Tawhid and Jihad, 20 June 2004.

'May your hand be strengthened!'—so said all those who
saw the video that showed the slaying of the Egyptian spy in
service of the American army in Iraq—I mean all those of
true faith. You are wrong if you think that it was only the
Egyptian spy who was slain. No, for among those who fell to
that happy dagger were a mighty infidel tyranny and an idol
who is worshipped instead of Allah; did you not see this as he
was slain?!

Abd al-Rahman ibn Salem al-Shamari, August-September
2004.

BIN LADEN, ATTEMPTS TO CAPTURE OR ASSASSINATE

There were several attempts to arrest me or to assassinate
me. This has been going on for more than seven years. With
Allah's grace, none of these attempts succeeded. This is proof
in itself to Muslims and to the world that the U.S. is incapable

and weaker than the picture it wants to draw in people's minds.

Osama bin Laden, March 1997.

An attempt on my life took place when the Saudi regime sent a number of people, who, though they were born in the Land of the Two Holy Mosques, were deprived of citizenship. The Saudi regime exploited this weakness and offered them large sums of money in return for trying to assassinate me.

By the grace of Allah, praise and glory be to Him, the Taliban were able to arrest one of them...He confessed that Prince Salman bin Abdel Aziz, the brother of the current king of the Land of the Two Holy Mosques, had promised to give him citizenship and a million rials if he was able, together with two other colleagues of his, to assassinate Osama bin Laden. We were not hurt. For us Allah suffices, and as I said lifetime is pre-ordained.

Osama bin Laden, 22 December 1998.

BIN LADEN, ON HIMSELF

I am one of Allah's worshippers. I worship Allah, which includes carrying out the jihad to raise Allah's word and to evict the Americans from all Muslim land.

Osama bin Laden, 28 May 1998.

If the instigation for jihad against the Jews and the Americans, in order to liberate the al-Aqsa Mosque and the holy Ka'ba, is considered a crime, let history be a witness that I am a criminal.

Osama bin Laden, 22 December 1998.

For the American forces to expect anything from me personally reflects a very narrow perception of things. There is a nation which compromises [millions of] Muslims. This nation is angry. The latest events have proven the great extent of the anger of the Muslim masses all over the Muslim world.

Osama bin Laden, 22 December 1998.

Allah was gracious enough for me to be born to Muslim parents in the Arabian Peninsula, in the al-Malazz neighborhood in Riyadh, in 1377 hegira [1957]. Then Allah was gracious to us as we went to holy Medina six months after I was born. For the rest of my life I stayed in Hejaz moving between Mecca, Jeddah and Medina.

As it is well known, my father, Sheikh Muhammad bin-'Awad bin-Laden, was born in Hadramaut. He went to work in Hejaz at an early age, more than 70 years ago. Then Allah blessed him and bestowed on him an honor that no other contractor has known. He built the holy Mecca mosque where the holy Ka'ba is located, and at the same time—because of Allah's blessings to him—he built the holy mosque in Medina for our Prophet, Allah's prayers be upon him.

Then when he found out that the government of Jordan announced a tender for restoration work on the Dome of the Rock Mosque, he gathered engineers and asked them to estimate the cost price only, without profit. They said to him: With Allah's help, we would be awarded the project and make some profit as well. He said to them: Calculate only the cost price of the project. When they did, they were surprised that he, Allah have mercy on his soul, reduced the cost price in order to guarantee that Allah's mosques, and this mosque in particular, were well served. He was awarded the project. Because of Allah's graciousness to him, sometimes he prayed in all three mosques in one single day. May Allah have mercy on his soul. It is not a secret that he was one of the founders of the infrastructure of the Kingdom of Saudi Arabia.

Afterward, I studied in Hejaz. I studied economy at Jeddah University, or the so-called King 'Abd-al-'Aziz University. I worked at an early age on roads in my father's company, may Allah have mercy on his soul. My father died when I was 10 years old.

Osama bin Laden, 10 June 1999.

The U.S. claims are numerous. If we presume that they are true, we are not concerned by them. These people are resisting the forces of world infidelity that occupied their lands. Why should the United States get angry when the people resist its aggressions? Its claims are baseless. However, if it means that I have something to do with instigating them, I would like to say that this is obvious. I have frequently admitted to having done so. I admitted that I was one of those who cosigned the fatwa that urged the Muslim community to engage in jihad.

Osama bin Laden, 10 June 1999.

America is against the establishment of any Islamic government. The Prophet has said, "They will be a target because of their religion." Not because Osama bin Laden is there.

Osama bin Laden, 21 October 2001.

BIN LADEN, SECRET MESSAGES

[America] made hilarious claims. They said that Osama's messages have codes in them to the terrorists. It's as if we were living in the time of mail by carrier pigeon, when there were no phones, no travelers, no Internet, no regular mail, no express mail and no electronic mail. I mean, these are very humorous things. They discount people's intellects.

Osama bin Laden, 21 October 2001.

BOSNIA

But the situation there [Bosnia] does not provide the same opportunities as Afghanistan. A small number of Mujahideen have gone to fight in Bosnia-Herzegovina, but the Croats won't allow the Mujahideen in through Croatia as the Pakistanis did with Afghanistan.

Osama bin Laden, 6 December 1993.

The Crusaders continued their slaughter of our mothers, sisters and children. America every time has made a decision to support them, to prevent weapons from reaching the Muslims, and to allow Serbian butchers to slaughter Muslims.

Osama bin Laden, 28 May 1998.

BUSH, GEORGE

Bush is an agent of Israel and sacrifices his people and his country's economy for them, and helps them occupy the Muslims' land and persecute their sons.

Sulaiman Abu Ghaith, 13 October 2001.

After the U.S. politicians spoke and after the U.S. newspapers and television channels became full of clear crusading hatred in this campaign that aims at mobilizing the West against Islam and Muslims, Bush left no room for doubts or the opinions of journalists, but he openly and clearly said that this war is a Crusader war. He said this before the whole world to emphasize this fact...The unequivocal truth is that

Bush has carried the cross and raised its banner high and stood at the front of the queue.

Osama bin Laden, 3 November 2001.

What Bush, the pharaoh of this age, was doing in terms of killing our sons in Iraq, and what Israel, the United States' ally, was doing in terms of bombing houses that shelter old people, women and children with U.S.-made aircraft in Palestine were sufficient to prompt the sane among your rulers to distance themselves from this criminal gang.

Osama bin Laden, 12 November 2002.

The Mujahideen saw that the gang of black-hearted criminals in the White House was misrepresenting the event [Al Qaeda attacks], and that that their leader [President Bush], who is a fool whom all obey, was claiming that we were jealous of their way of life, while the truth—which the Pharaoh of our generation conceals—is that we strike at them because of the way they oppress us in the Muslim world, especially in Palestine and Iraq, and because of their occupation of the Land of the Two Holy Mosques. When the Mujahideen saw this they decided to act in secret and to move the battle right into his [President Bush's] country and his own territory.

Osama bin Laden, 11 February 2003.

Bush, the son of Bush, is a dog and the son of a dog; his blood is the blood of a dog; his bark is the bark of a dog; and he has all the traits of a dog except for loyalty. Thus, he is a hyena.

Sheikh Nasser al-Najdi, October 2003.

Bush and his gang, with their heavy sticks and hard hearts, are an evil to all humankind. They have stabbed into the truth, until they have killed it altogether in the eyes of the world. With this behavior they have encouraged hypocrisy, and spread vice and political bribes shamelessly at the level of heads of state. This gang and their leader enjoy lying, war and looting to serve their own ambitions...Thanks be to Allah, who has exposed the lies of George Bush and made his term as president a term of continual catastrophe. To Bush I say, you are begging the world to come to your aid, begging mercenaries from every corner of the world, even from small states. This begging has destroyed your pride and revealed how trivial and weak you are after claiming to defend the whole world.

Osama bin Laden, 18 October 2003.

As for you, Bush, dog of the Christians, we promise you things that will displease you. With Allah's assistance, hard days are coming to you. You and your soldiers are going to regret the day that you stepped foot in Iraq and dared to violate Muslims.

Abu Mus'ab al-Zarqawi, 11 May 2004.

[The results of the war so far have] surpassed all expectations by all criteria for many reasons, one of the most important of which is that we had no difficulty dealing with Bush and his administration, because it resembles the regimes in our [Arab] countries, half of which are ruled by the military, and the other half are ruled by the sons of kings and presidents with whom we have had a lot of experience. Among both types, there are many who are known for their conceit, arrogance, greed and for taking money unrightfully.

Osama bin Laden, 29 October 2004.

Bush's hands are sullied with the blood of all of these casualties on both sides, for the sake of oil and to give business to his private companies.

Osama bin Laden, 29 October 2004.

CELL PHONES

Use a cell phone only when you must, and an alternative means of communication is not available...it is better not to use cell phones at all...if you must use a cell phone, use one obtained under a fake name and address...never use a phone provided by your leader for calling a friend or relative...if you ask your friends to call you, given them a specific time and keep your phone open only when you are expecting a call...Do not receive a phone at your residence, do so at a bazaar or at an open space and shut off the phone and disconnect the battery as soon as you finish the conversation.

Al Qaeda, January 2004.

CENSORSHIP, WESTERN

It became a total mockery and that clearly appeared when the U.S. government interfered and banned the media outlets from airing our words, which don't exceed a few minutes, because they felt the truth had started to appear to the American people, and that we truly aren't terrorists by the definition they want, but because we are being violated in Palestine, in Iraq, in Lebanon, in Sudan, in Somalia, in Kashmir, in the Philippines, and in every place...Therefore, they declared what they declared and ordered what they ordered, and they forgot everything they mentioned about free speech, unbiased opinion and all those matters. So I say that freedom and rights in America, and human rights, have been sent forward to the guillotine with no return unless they are quickly reinstated.

Osama bin Laden, 23 May 2002

CHECHNYA

The West, and the rest of the world, are accusing Osama bin Laden of being the prime sponsor and organizer of what they call 'international terrorism' today. But as far as we are concerned, he is our brother in Islam. He is someone with knowledge and a Mujahid fighting with his wealth and his self for the sake of Allah. He is a sincere brother, and he is completely the opposite to what the disbelievers are accusing him of. We know that he is well established with the Mujahideen in Afghanistan and other places in the world. What the Americans are saying is not true. However, it is an obligation for all Muslims to help each other in order to promote the religion of Islam. Osama bin Laden is one of the major scholars of the jihad, as well as being a main commander of the Mujahideen worldwide. He fought for many years against the Communists in Afghanistan and now is engaged in a war against American imperialism.

Omar ibn al-Khattab, 27 September 1999.

They [the Chechens] are a Muslim people who have been attacked by the Russian bear which embraces the Christian Orthodox faith. The Russians annihilated the Chechen people in their entirety and forced them to flee to the mountains where they were assaulted by snow, poverty and diseases. Nonetheless, nobody moved to support them... The entire Chechen people are being embattled once again by this Russian bear. The humanitarian agencies, even the U.S. ones, demanded that President Clinton should stop supporting Russia. However, Clinton said that stopping support for Russia did not serve U.S. interests. A year ago, [Russian President] Putin demanded that the cross and the Jews should stand by him. He told them: You must support us and thank us because we are waging a war against Muslim fundamentalism.

Osama bin Laden, 3 November 2001.

The Chechen Mujahideen, together with their Muslim brethren, deflated the Russians' pride and caused them loss after loss. Beaten, they withdrew after the first war. Later the Russians returned with American support, and Russia is still suffering heavy losses because of a small group of believers, whom, we pray, Allah will support and make victorious.

Osama bin Laden, 11 February 2003.

CIVILIANS, KILLING OF

We say that the prohibition against the blood of women, children, and the elderly is not an absolute prohibition. Rather, there are special conditions in which it is permissible to kill them if they are among the people of war, and these conditions exist in specific circumstances. We say that a number of protected people were among the victims of the September [2001] operations in America, but they do not fall outside the conditions that permit killing them...

First: It is allowed for Muslims to kill protected ones among unbelievers as an act of reciprocity. If the unbelievers have targeted Muslim women, children and elderly, it is permissible for Muslims to respond in kind and kill those similar to those whom the unbelievers killed...

Second: It is allowed for Muslims to kill protected ones among unbelievers in the event of an attack against them in which it is not possible to differentiate the protected ones from the combatants or from the strongholds...

Third: It is allowed for Muslims to kill protected ones among unbelievers on the condition that the protected ones have assisted in combat, whether in deed, word, mind, or any other form of assistance...

Fourth: It is allowed for Muslims to kill protected ones among unbelievers in the event of a need to burn the strongholds or fields of the enemy so as to weaken its strength in order to conquer the stronghold or topple the state...

Fifth: It is allowed for Muslims to kill protected ones among unbelievers when they are using heavy weapons that do not distinguish between combatants and protected ones...

Sixth: It is allowed for Muslims to kill protected ones among unbelievers when the enemy is shielded by their women and children. If it is not possible to engage in battle and hold back their evil from the land of Islam, it is the consensus that it is permissible for them to kill the human shields.

Seventh: It is allowed for Muslims to kill protected ones among unbelievers if the people of a treaty violate their treaty, and the leader must kill them in order to teach them a lesson.

Al Qaeda, 24 April 2002.

CLERICS, MUSLIM

Most unfortunately, the young people who have the ability to sacrifice [themselves] for the religion are suffering by listening to and obeying Islamic clerics who refrain [from fulfilling the commandment of jihad]...

Great evil is spreading throughout the Islamic world: the imams calling people to hell are those who appear more than others at the side of rulers in the region, the rulers of the Arab and Islamic world. Through the media and their own apparatuses, through their ruin of the country by their adoption of destructive ideas, and laws created by man...from morning to evening, they call the people to the gates of hell...

They [clerics]...are busy handing out praise and words of glory to the despotic Arab rulers who have disbelieved Allah and His Prophet. They send telegrams praising those rulers who disbelieve Allah and His Prophet. Their newspapers and media spread heresy against Allah and His Prophet. Other telegrams are sent from the rulers to these clerics, praising them for deceiving the Muslim community.

Osama bin Laden, July 2003.

I have looked over the list of the martyrs and of their history, and I was most regretful to find among them not a single cleric from among the clerics of the Muslim community whose books fill the libraries. I found not a single preacher from among the preachers who have filled the world with their cassettes in which they spoke of the reward of jihad and its status in the eyes of Allah. In my mind arose many questions for which I have found no answers. Why do the clerics, the sheikhs, and the preachers not aspire to gain the reward of jihad and the status of martyrs next to Allah? Don't they need this reward and status? Or does their role end with the spoken word or the written letter? Allah will call them tomorrow to account for this [on the Day of Judgment].

Muhammad bin Shazzaf al-Shahri, 17 October 2003.

The false Islamic clerics and mercenary writers [in Saudi Arabia] turn wherever the ruler turns, and they fall in with him wherever he falls in for the sake of money, and [yet] they still claim religious knowledge and wisdom and guidance and uprightness.

Osama bin Laden, 27 December 2004.

CLINTON, WILLIAM

The hearts of Muslims are filled with hatred towards the United States of America and the American president. The president has a heart that knows no words. A heart that kills hundreds of children definitely knows no words. Our people in the Arabian Peninsula will send him messages with no words because he does not know any words.

Osama bin Laden, March 1997.

To these [American] mothers I say if they are concerned for their sons, then let them object to the American government's policy and to the American president. Do not let yourselves be cheated by his standing before the bodies of the killed soldiers describing the Mujahideen in Saudi Arabia as terrorists. It is he who is a terrorist who pushed their sons into this for the sake of Israeli interests.

Osama bin Laden, March 1997.

If the Americans kill little children in Palestine and innocents in Iraq, and if the majority of Americans support that perverted president [Bill Clinton], that means that the American people are at war with us and that we have the right to take them as targets.

Osama bin Laden, 22 December 1998.

Clinton is a target for jihad, and American forces are a target for the jihad wherever they are...the American people must reconsider their foreign policy, or their children will be sent back to them in coffins.

Sheikh Omar bin Bakri Muhammad, 30 May 2000.

CLINTON, WILLIAM, FAILED ASSASSINATION ATTEMPT (1995)

Wali Khan is a Muslim youth. In Afghanistan, he is nicknamed "The Lion." He is one of the best youths. We were good friends. We fought together in the same trench against the Russians until Allah sent them away in humiliating defeat. You mentioned that he works for me—we do not have anyone who works for someone else. We all work for Allah and await his reward. And regarding your mention of his attempt to assassinate President Clinton, it is not surprising. I did not know about it, but it is not surprising. As I said, every action solicits a similar reaction. What does Clinton expect from those whom he killed and assaulted their children and mothers? This is not a surprising matter.

Osama bin Laden, 28 May 1998.

CLINTON ADMINISTRATION

I say that the American people gave leadership to a traitorous leadership. This became very clear and especially in Clinton's government. The American government, we think, is an agent that represents the Israelis inside America. If we look at sensitive departments in the present government, like the Department of Defense or the State Department, or sensitive security departments like the CIA and others, we find that Jews have the first word in the American government, which is how they use America to carry out their plans in the world and especially the Muslim world.

Osama bin Laden, 28 May 1998.

COLE, USS, ATTACK ON (12 OCTOBER 2000)

The courage of our youth was witnessed in Aden, where they destroyed their destroyer and instilled fear...Their ships stand so arrogantly in our ports.

Osama bin Laden, 20 June 2001.

The recent operations were meant to support the jihad in Palestine against the Jewish enemy. We said at the time that the operations against the [USS] *Cole* was the first serious attack in support of the Palestinian uprising, and it would be followed by sister operations.

Al Qaeda, 26 April 2002.

A watch was established on the [USS *Cole*] destroyer for a while during which time information was gathered by the 'Committees for Intelligence-Gathering.' Only two people worked on this, no more and no less. The allegations that the Mossad was responsible [for the attack on the *Cole*] are nonsense and are an attempt to cast doubt on the ability of the Muslims to do something of this sort. Those who carried out the operation were well-known young men from among the ranks of our brothers the Mujahideen...

There were many reasons: [we wanted to] damage the U.S.A's reputation in the naval arena, to raise the morale of the Muslims, and to prove to the Muslim community that its sons are capable of striking the Muslim community's enemies wherever they may be, by sea, by air, and by land...Nearly 71 Islamic countries are incapable of saying 'no' to the U.S. but as individuals we can say 'no' to it...The choice of the best destroyer in the American navy and the best product of the American military was a difficult blow for the U.S., [which proves that] we are capable of striking them whenever we see fit and in any manner that we see fit.

Nasser Ahmad Nasser al-Bahri, 3 August 2004.

DEMOCRACY

America is the head of heresy in our modern world, and it leads an infidel democratic regime that is based upon separation of religion and state, and on ruling the people by the people via legislating laws that contradict the way of Allah and permit what Allah has prohibited.

Sulaiman Abu Ghaith, 12 June 2002.

Voices have risen in Iraq as before in Palestine, Egypt, Jordan, Yemen and elsewhere, calling for a peaceful democratic solution in dealing with apostate governments or with Jewish and Crusader invaders instead of fighting in the name of Allah. Hence, it is necessary to warn against the danger of this deviant and misleading practice that contradicts Allah's teachings to fight in the name of Allah...They have chosen democracy, the faith of the ignorant, through becoming members of legislative councils...

Islam is the faith of Allah, while the legislative councils are the faith of the ignorant. Those who obey their kings or scholars—in permitting what Allah has prohibited, such as becoming members of the legislative councils, or prohibiting what Allah has permitted, such as jihad for the sake of Allah— they have thus made them their lords, rather than obey Allah.

Osama bin Laden, 18 October 2003.

Your jihad [in Iraq] against the Crusaders is in defense of Islam, whose enemies are aiming to remove it from the hearts and lives of the Muslims. In this crime of democracy, the ones aiding them [the Allied forces] are members of our people and those who speak in their name, who call their apostasy and corruption 'reform'...Democracy [in Iraq] is a victory for the Crusaders, even if they retreat from Iraq and leave their agents to guard the idol of democracy that has become the god worshipped instead of Allah.

Sheikh Abu Omar al-Sayf, December 2004.

Democracy is based on the principle that the people are the source of all authority...In other words, the legislator who must be obeyed in a democracy is man, and not Allah. That means that the one who is worshipped and obeyed and deified, from the point of view of legislating and prohibiting, is man, the created, and not Allah. That is the very essence of heresy and polytheism and error...

Under democracy, a man can believe anything he wants, choose any religion he wants, and convert to any religion whenever he wants, even if this apostasy means abandoning the religion of Allah...This is a matter which is patently perverse and false...

Democracy is based on the principal of 'freedom of expression,' no matter what the expression might be, even if it means hurting and reviling the Divine Being [Allah] and the laws of Islam, because in democracy nothing is so sacred that one cannot be insolent or use vile language about it.

Democracy is based on the principle of freedom of association and of forming political parties and the like, no matter what the creed, ideas, and ethics of these parties may be... voluntary recognition of the legality of heretical parties implies acquiescence in heresy...Acquiescence in heresy is heresy...

Democracy is based on the principle of considering the position of the majority and adopting what is agreed upon by the majority, even if they agree upon falsehood, error, and blatant heresy.

Abu Mus'ab al-Zarqawi, 23 January 2005.

Democracy and parliaments, my brothers, are from the religion and desires of infidels...Democracy means the rule of the people...which means that who is to be obeyed and worshipped is not Allah.

Abu Maysara, 2 March 2005.

DETERRENCE

Deterrence: This principle is based on the assumption that there are two sides that seek to survive and defend their interests—but it is completely eliminated when dealing with people who don't care about living but thirst for martyrdom. While the principle works well [in warfare] between countries, it does not work at all for an organization with no permanent bases and with no capital in Western banks, that does not rely on aid from particular countries. As a result, it is completely independent in its decisions, and it seeks conflict from the outset. How can such people, who strive for death more than anything else, be deterred?

Abu Ubayd al-Qurashi, January/February 2002.

DOGS

Dogs, like other animals, are not assigned [religious] missions and commandments, and [religious prohibitions] are not forbidden them; they were created according to a particular nature, and they do not deviate from their nature. They are different from the infidel, who was created by Allah in order to worship Him and in order to believe in His monotheism, but who denied Him, and took other gods beside Him. Anyone who is satisfied with what is said above concludes that the heresy of that infidel and his rebellion against the religion of Allah requires the permitting of his blood and [sanctions] his humiliation, and that his blood is like the blood of a dog and nothing more.

Sheikh Nasser al-Najdi, October 2003.

ECONOMIC STRATEGY OF AL QAEDA

The first thing is that Western products could only be boycotted when the Muslim fraternity is fully awakened and organized. Secondly, the Muslim companies should become self-sufficient in producing goods equal to the products of Western companies. Economic boycott of the West is not possible unless economic self-sufficiency is attained and substitute products are brought out.

Osama bin Laden, 28 September 2001.

There is another way through hitting the [U.S.] economic structure, which is basic for military power. If their economy is destroyed, they will be busy with their own affairs rather than enslaving the weak peoples. It is very important to concentrate on hitting the U.S. economy through all possible means.

Osama bin Laden, 26 December 2001.

The youth of Islam are preparing things that will fill your hearts with fear. They will target key sectors of your economy until you stop your injustice and aggression or until the more short-lived of us die.

Osama bin Laden, 6 October 2002.

A conviction has formed among the Mujahideen that American public opinion is not the center of gravity in America. The Zionist lobbies, and with them the security agencies, have long been able to bridle all the media that control the formation of public opinion in America. This time it is clearly apparent that the American economy is the American center of gravity...Supporting this strategic view is that the Disunited States of America are a mixture of nationalities, ethnic groups, and races united only by the "American Dream," or, to put it more correctly, worship of the dollar...the entire American war effort is based on pumping enormous wealth at all times, money being, as has been said, the sinew of war.

Abu Ubayd al-Qurashi, 10 December 2002.

The final blows in the crucial battles are at hand. We are now living in crucial days and we are seeing how the government of the idol of this age [the U.S.] is filled with fear and dread, dreaming of obtaining security and calm, and spending a billion dollars every week in order to protect itself from the imminent unknown danger coming from the direction [of the enemy] that they claimed to have completely destroyed years ago.

Abu Abd al-Rahman al-Turkemani, December 2003.

The purpose of these targets [economic targets] is to destabilize the situation and not allow the economic recovery, such as hitting oil wells and pipelines that will scare foreign companies from working there and stealing Muslim treasures. Another purpose is to have foreign investment withdrawn from local markets. Some of the benefits of those operations are the effect it has on the economic powers, like the one that happened recently in Madrid, where the whole European economy suffered. Such attacks have dual economic effects on the Crusaders, Jewish and renegade Islamic countries.

Abdul Aziz al-Muqrin, 29 March 2004.

As previously mentioned, it was easy for us to provoke this administration and to drag it [after us]. It was enough for us to send two jihad fighters to the farthest east to hoist a rag on which 'Al Qaeda' was written—that was enough to cause generals to rush off to this place, thereby causing America human and financial and political losses, without it accomplishing anything worthy of mention, apart from giving business to [the generals'] private corporations. Besides, we gained experience in guerilla warfare and in conducting a war of attrition in our fight with the iniquitous, great power, that is, when we conducted a war of attrition against Russia with jihad fighters for 10 years until they went bankrupt, with Allah's grace; as a result, they were forced to withdraw in defeat, all praise and thanks to Allah. We are continuing in the same policy—to make America bleed profusely to the point of bankruptcy, Allah willing.

Osama bin Laden, 29 October 2004.

The Mujahideen have finally forced Bush to have recourse to an emergency budget in order to continue the fight in Afghanistan and Iraq, which indicates the success of the plan to exhaust [them] to the point of bankruptcy, Allah willing.

Al-Battar, 10 November 2004.

EGYPT

The Islamic Group in Egypt has established a true struggle which has been able to oppose the oppressive regime in Egypt and to turn the attention of the world to the extent of the tyranny under which the Egyptian people suffer...The reality is that the Egyptian regime did not just participate in the destruction which took place in Egypt, the Egyptian regime is destruction itself...The Islamic state in Egypt is coming, the rate of its approaching is increasing day after day.

Abu-Yasir Rifa'i Ahmad Taha, April-May 1997.

Our officers and soldiers, and the sons of our people in

Egypt, should learn the lesson of the U.S. destroyer in Aden; they have the Suez Canal through which dozens of U.S. and Jewish ships pass...They [Jews and Americans] must realize that we have no other option but to besiege their embassies and military and civilian centers in our countries, which are numerous...let the embassies and centers be burned down, ships and destroyers destroyed and individuals killed.

Abu-Yasir Rifa'i Ahmad Taha, 18 October 2000.

ENEMIES

Our enemy, the target—if Allah gives Muslims the opportunity to do so—is every American male, whether he is directly fighting us or paying taxes.

Osama bin Laden, 10 June 1999.

Fighting them [the Americans] is an obligation in which there can be no compromise, until they leave the Arabian Peninsula and all the Muslim lands they occupy.

Sulaiman Abu Ghaith, 10 July 2001.

What do the Arab countries have to do with this Crusade? Everyone who supports Bush, even with one word, commits an act of great treason.

Osama bin Laden, 21 October 2001.

Our solution is organized jihad that sets at the head of its priorities the attack against American and Zionist interests. It should not just boycott their goods, but explode their headquarters, centers, and industries, and everything that symbolizes them, such as McDonald's etc. We should add to that the killing of Americans and Zionists, and their loyal agents, in order that they will not feel safe anywhere in the Muslim world, and return to their homelands leaving the Muslim countries to their real owners.

Abu Ayman al-Hilali, May 2002.

Nothing will do you [Muslims] good, but toting arms and taking revenge against your enemies, the Americans and the Jews...The Crusaders and the Jews only understand the language of killing and blood. They do not become convinced unless they see coffins returning to them, their interests being destroyed, their towers being torched, and their economy collapsing. O Muslims, take matters firmly against the embassies of America, England, Australia, and Norway and their interests, companies and employees. Burn the ground under their feet.

Ayman al-Zawahiri, 21 May 2003.

Our number-one enemy is the Jews and the Christians, and we must make ourselves available and invest all our effort until we destroy them—and we are capable of doing this if

Allah allows us to—because they are the main obstacle to the establishment of the Islamic state.

Sulaiman al-Dosari, *The Voice of Jihad*, no. 2, October 2003.

The Jews, the Americans and Crusaders in general will remain the targets of our coming attacks...And the apostate Saudi government will be incapable of protecting their interests of providing security for them...We warn Muslims to stay away from Americans and their civilian and military sites so that they will not be harmed when the infidels are targeted...We reiterate our previous declared commitment of the jihad policy of Al Qaeda to target the Crusaders, Jews and apostates.

Abdul Aziz al-Muqrin, 27 April 2004.

Ever since the beginning of creation, there has been a conflict between truth and falsehood, [and this will continue] until Allah inherits the earth and everyone on it...Another chapter of this conflict is taking place now in Iraq, represented by the worshippers of the Cross [Christians], and they have openly declared it to be a Crusade.

Abu Mus'ab al-Zarqawi, 18 May 2005.

ESPIONAGE

Spying on the enemy is permitted, and it may even be a duty in the case of war between Muslims and others. Winning the battle is dependent on knowing the enemy's secrets, movements and plans...How can a Muslim spy live among enemies if he maintains his Islamic characteristics? How can he perform his duties to Allah and not want to appear Muslim? Concerning the issue of clothing and appearance... resembling the polytheist in religious appearance is a kind of 'necessity permits the forbidden,' even though they [forbidden acts] are basically prohibited. As for the visible duties, like fasting and praying, he can fast by using any justification not to eat with them [polytheists]. As for prayer,...[the Muslim] may combine the noon and afternoon [prayers], sunset and evening [prayers]...It is noted, however, that it is forbidden to do the unlawful, such as drinking wine or fornicating. There is nothing that permits those.

Al Qaeda, 10 May 2000.

Measures that Should be Taken by the Undercover Member: 1) Not reveal his true name to the Organization's members who are working with him; 2) Have a general appearance that does not indicate Islamic orientation (beard, toothpick, book, [long] shirt, small *Qur'an*); 3) Be careful not to mention the brothers' common expressions or show their behavior...; 4) Avoid visiting famous Islamic places (mosques, libraries, Islamic fairs, etc.).

Al Qaeda, 10 May 2000.

When you work in a group, each person knows only what he is supposed to do, not more, to preserve your secrets. Avoid the places that are suspicious or will bring suspicion upon you, such as mosques. Avoid wearing clothing that would bring suspicion upon you. When you speak on the phone, speak in a very natural, normal language, or in a foreign language.

Ahmed Ressam, July 2001.

Every member will take all necessary precautions in his personal and social life to protect the group and its leadership... in his personal life, each member shall merge completely with the society he lives in so that he is indistinguishable from other members of the society...If you live in an area where people wear Western dress, you also dress like them ...if the majority in that area has a secular mindset, do not express your religious sentiments...

Look closely at the ethnic complexion of your neighborhood...if the area has a large number of people from ethnic groups that support the government, stay away from them because they often spy for intelligence agencies...Don't visit the local mosque regularly. Instead say your prayers at your residence...Don't roam around with beard and Islamic dress in fashionable neighborhoods.

Always take out the chip of the mobile [phone] while sleeping to avoid being caught. Use mobile [phones] from a crowded place so police don't locate the position. Don't write the original numbers of Mujahideen in a notebook; try to memorize the last three digits...If you live in an area where people do not have cars, avoid using vehicles...if you have to stay inside your residence when other people go to work, be quiet. Do not draw attention...Know your neighbors but do not make too many friends...do not travel unless you have to...do not visit new cities and countries...never keep illegal objects while traveling...never carry audio or video cassettes and posters of your group or leader while traveling.

Al Qaeda, January 2004.

On arriving at a new zone the following method should be observed: obtain the local telephone directly, tourist maps and newspapers, change your outward guise, avoid places where you may be exposed to danger, familiarize yourself with the local standards of security, culture, society, ethics and services.

Al-Battar, 10 November 2004.

EUROPE

Today we declare the start of a bloody war on you [European governments], and we will not stop the attacks on you until you return to the correct path...We will make the blood flow so deep that it will sweep you away...we will shake the cities of Europe...O' leaders and peoples of Europe, remove your murderous forces from Iraq...before you begin to taste the bitterness of your own blood.

Abu Hafs al-Masri Brigades, 28 July 2004.

EUROPE, BIN LADEN OFFERS A TRUCE TO

Examining the developments that have been taking place, in terms of killings in our countries and your countries, will make clear an important fact; namely, that injustice is inflicted on us and on you by your politicians, who send your sons—although you are opposed to this—to our countries to kill and be killed.Therefore, it is in both sides' interest to curb the plans of those who shed the blood of peoples for their narrow personal interest and subservience to the White House gang...

I...offer a reconciliation initiative...whose essence is our commitment to stopping operations against every country that commits itself to not attacking Muslims or interfering in their affairs—including the U.S. conspiracy on the greater Muslim world...The reconciliation will start with the departure of [your] last soldier from our country. The door of reconciliation is open for three months of the date of announcing this statement. For those who reject reconciliation and want war, we are ready. As for those who want reconciliation, we have given them a chance. Stop shedding our blood so as to preserve your blood...You know the situation will expand and increase if you delay.

Osama bin Laden, 15 April 2004.

EUROPE, IRAQ WAR

We emphasize that a withdrawal of the Spanish or Italian forces from Iraq would put huge pressure on the British presence [in Iraq], a pressure that [Prime Minister] Tony Blair might not be able to withstand, and hence the domino tiles would fall quickly. Yet, the basic problem of making the first tile fall still remains.

Sheikh Yousef al-Ayiri, 10 December 2003.

FINANCES

Financial Security Precautions: 1) Dividing operational funds into two parts: one part is to be invested in projects that offer financial return, and the other is to be saved and not spent except during operations; 2) Not placing operational funds [all] in one place; 3) Not telling the organization members about the location of the funds; 4) Having proper protection while carrying large amounts of money; and 5) Leaving the money with non-members and spending it as needed.

Al Qaeda, 10 May 2000.

FINANCES, EFFORTS TO IMPEDE AL QAEDA'S

Our livelihood is set. No matter how much pressure America places on the regime in Riyadh to freeze our assets and to prevent people from contributing to this great cause, we rely on Allah.

Osama bin Laden, 28 May 1998.

The freezing of accounts will not make any difference for Al Qaeda or other jihad groups. With the grace of Allah, Al Qaeda has more than three alternative financial systems, which are all separate and totally independent from each other. This system is operating under the patronage of those who love jihad...Al Qaeda is comprised of modern, educated youths who are as aware of the cracks inside the Western financial system as they are aware of the lines in their hands.

Osama bin Laden, 28 September 2001.

FOREIGN FIGHTERS IN IRAQ

The infidels once again are claiming that foreign fighters are responsible for initiating the attacks and an increase [in their numbers] is the true danger. However, we inform you, O' enemies of Allah, that the real danger is the increase [in numbers] of the followers of [Al Qaeda in Iraq], who love martyrdom and who stride towards paradise...Who is the foreigner, O' cross worshippers? You are the ones who came to the land of the Muslims from your distant corrupt land. However, do not worry because the swords of the Mujahideen and the spears of the martyrs will be waiting for you.

Al Qaeda in Iraq, 10 May 2005.

FRANCE

This [French veil ban] is a new sign of the Crusader hatred which Westerners harbor against Muslims while they boast of freedom, democracy and human rights. France is the country of freedom which defends freedom to show the body, and to be immoral and depraved. In France you're free to show yourself but not to dress modestly.

Ayman al-Zawahiri, 24 February 2004.

France has distinguished itself for its war against Islam and Muslims and has committed butchery against the Muslim community...France's history with Muslims is a black one, blemished by hatred and malice and blood. Its modern history is no less so than in the past.

Islamic Army of Iraq, 15 September 2004.

FREEDOM

The freedom that we want is not the freedom of interest-bearing banks and vast corporations and misleading mass media; not the freedom of the destruction of others for the sake of materialistic interests; and not the freedom of AIDS and an industry of obscenities and homosexual marriages; and not the freedom to use women as a commodity to gain clients, win deals, or attract tourists; not the freedom of Hiroshima and Nagasaki; and not the freedom of trading in the apparatus of torture and supporting the regimes of oppression and Copts

[Egypt's Christian minority] and suppression, the friends of America; and not the freedom of Israel, with their annihilation of the Muslims and destruction of the al-Aqsa mosque; and not the freedom of Guantanamo and Abu Ghraib.

Our freedom is a freedom of monotheism and morals and probity and asceticism and justice. The freedom that we are striving toward is based on three foundations: The first is the rule of the Shari'a...The second foundation, upon which reform must be established... is the freedom of the lands of Islam and their liberation from every robbing and looting aggressor. It is unimaginable that any reform may be realized for us while we are under the coercion of American and Jewish occupation.... As for the third foundation...it is the liberation of man. The Muslim community must snatch back its right to choose its ruler and call him to account and criticize him and depose him...The Muslim community must undertake [to end] repression and brute force and theft and fraud and corruption and dynastic succession in rule, which our rulers are practicing with the blessings and support of the United States.

Ayman al-Zawahiri, 30 January 2005.

GOALS

We seek to instigate the Muslim community to get up and liberate its land, to fight for the sake of Allah, and to make the Shari'a the highest law, and the word of Allah the highest word of all.

Osama bin Laden, 10 June 1999.

The main mission for which the Military Organization is responsible is: The overthrow of the godless regimes and their replacement with an Islamic regime.

Al Qaeda, 10 May 2000.

The liberation of our holy places and countries, first and foremost Palestine and the Land of the Two Holy Mosques, is our primary goal for which all efforts and forces must unite. It is the issue that demands all the Muslims, apart from their different races and languages and colors, to work for it as the Muslims are like one body.

Sulaiman Abu Ghaith, 7 December 2002.

We want from all Christians and Jews to go out from our Islamic countries, release our brothers from jails, and stop killing Muslims, or we will kill you as you are killing Muslims.

Muhammad bin Abd al-Wahhab al-Maqit, 17 October 2003.

Our war with the enemies of Allah continues everywhere... We will not let the Americans occupy the Land of the Two Holy

Mosques...and we will not cease our jihad until we liberate every inch of Muslim land.

Sulaiman al-Dosari, *The Voice of Jihad*, no. 2, October 2003.

There is no doubt that the demise of America and its collapse will lead to the collapse of these fragile regimes that depend on it...We will not stop until we establish the Islamic Caliphate and until Allah's law is implemented in His land.

Abu Salma al-Hijazi, 14 November 2003.

The Al Qaeda organization's goal from its inception is to sow conflict between the United States and the Islamic world. I remember that Sheikh Osama bin Laden used to say that we can not, as an organization, continue in large-scale operations, but rather we must aspire to commit operations that will drag the United States into a regional confrontation with the Islamic peoples.

Nasser Ahmad Nasser al-Bahri, 3 August 2004.

GREAT BRITAIN

The real motive seems to be British Crusader hatred against Muslims and the appeasement of the Americans, which has become a distinctive feature of British foreign policy, as demonstrated by Britain's blind support of the hostile stands against Muslim peoples on more than one occasion. Britain's support of the U.S. aggression against Sudan and Afghanistan recently and the U.S. policy against the besieged Iraqi people is nothing but an indication of this orientation of this policy. Does Britain want to put itself in the same corner as the United States?

Osama bin Laden, 1 October 1998.

Now that the Americans, the British, and it is safe to assume, also the French, have begun to bomb Muslims in Afghanistan, government buildings here [in Britain], military installations, and No. 10 Downing Street have become legitimate targets. This also means Prime Minister Tony Blair has become a legitimate target. If any Muslim wants to kill him or get rid of him, I would not shed a tear for him. In the Islamic view, such a man would not be punished for his deeds, but would be praised.

Abd al-Rahman Salim, 10 October 2001.

[To Prime Minister Tony Blair] We say with confidence, that the worst of the incoming [attacks] hasn't happened yet, and that the West will pay a high price for all the crimes they committed against the Muslims during and before this century...When you invaded Iraq, you thought that it would be a picnic, [now you] find out today that in Falujah, Baquba, Ramadi...that [the Mujahideen] are the victorious.

Louis Attiyah Allah, May 2005.

GREATER ISRAEL

Their [Western forces] presence has no meaning save one and that is to offer support to the Jews in Palestine who are in need of their Christian brothers to achieve full control over the Arabian Peninsula which they intend to make an important part of the so-called 'Greater Israel.'

Osama bin Laden, 28 May 1998.

One of the most important objectives of the new Crusader attack is to pave the way and prepare the region, after its fragmentation, for the establishment of what is known as 'the Greater State of Israel,' whose border will include extensive areas of Iraq and Egypt, through Syria, Lebanon, Jordan, all of Palestine and large parts of the Land of the Two Holy Mosques.

Osama bin Laden, 11 February 2003.

GUANTANAMO, CUBA

What is happening at Guantanamo is a historical embarrassment to America and its values, and it screams into your faces—you hypocrites, "What is the value of your signature on any agreement or treaty?"

Al Qaeda, 24 November 2002.

You who shirk jihad, what excuse can you give Allah while your brethren in the prisons of Abu Ghraib and Guantanamo and Al-Ruways and Al-Ha'ir are stripped naked?

Abu Abd al-Rahman al-Athari Sultan ibn Bijad, 17 November 2004.

GUERRILLA WARFARE

Due to the imbalance of power between our armed forces and the enemy forces, a suitable means of fighting must be adopted, i.e. using fast-moving light forces that work under complete secrecy. In other words, to initiate guerrilla warfare, where the sons of the nation, and not the military forces, take part in it.

Osama bin Laden, 23 August 1996.

We are determined to defend ourselves, to fight a guerrilla war and to broaden this guerrilla war to all areas of Afghanistan. We stand on our right of self-defense.

Taliban Military Commander, 2 April 2002.

We, the Mujahideen in general, are getting ready to begin the next phase in what is termed in military science the phase of guerrilla warfare. We are trying to develop the fronts, where fighting is marked by skirmishes. We are now developing the fronts along all lines to make it a large-scale war—the war of ambushes, assassinations, and operations that take place in the most unexpected places to the enemy. We are succeeding in that, thanks to Allah's graces and the cohesion, affiliation, solidarity of the Mujahideen, both Arab and Afghan...We have also succeeded in reaching the phase of destroying bases and ammunition dumps and carrying out combat operations and assassinations.

Abu Laith al-Libi, 9 July 2002.

We would like to say to those who are rushing to victory that the kind of war carried on by the Mujahideen depends on a lengthy duration of time and depleting, exhausting and terrorizing the enemy and does not depend on adhering to the land...Converting the military force to small units with good administrative capabilities will save us from heavy losses at one hand, and also help in controlling all the fronts with the least possible number of personnel. In addition, converting the people to armed militias will render the mission of the enemy impossible.

Saif al-Adel, March 2003.

This [guerrilla warfare] is the most powerful weapon Muslims have, and it is the best method to continue the conflict with the Crusader enemy who has stripped the Muslim community of all the means of [military] might, and there is no chance that in the years to come we will be allowed to possess the elements of strength...the most effective method for the materially weak against the strong is guerrilla warfare.

Al Qaeda, 9 April 2003.

HINDUS

The Hindus were terrorists yesterday, they are terrorists today, and they will remain terrorists tomorrow. We are right in seeking revenge from these spawns of evil.

Hafiz Muhammad Saeed, February 2003.

HISTORY

After the fall of our orthodox caliphates on March 3, 1924, and after expelling the colonialists, our Islamic nation was afflicted with apostate rulers who took over in the Muslim nation. These rulers turned out to be more infidel and criminal than the colonialists themselves. Muslims have endured all kinds of harm, oppression, and torture at their hands... Colonialism and its followers, the apostate rulers, then started to openly erect Crusader centers, societies, and organizations like Masonic Lodges, Lions and Rotary Clubs, and foreign schools. They aimed at producing a wasted generation that pursued everything that is Western.

Al Qaeda, 10 May 2000.

In 1989, some American military experts predicted a fundamental change in the future form of warfare...They predicted that the wars of the 21st century would be dominated by a kind of warfare they called 'the fourth generation of wars.' Others called it 'asymmetric warfare'...

This new type of war presents significant difficulties for the Western war machine, and it can be expected that [Western] armies will change fundamentally. This forecast did not arise in a vacuum—if only the cowards [among the Muslim clerics] knew that fourth-generation wars have already occurred and that the superiority of the theoretically weaker party has already been proven; in many instances, nation-states have been defeated by stateless nations...

The Muslim community has chalked up the most victories in a short time...These victories were achieved during the past twenty years, against the best armed, best trained, and most experienced armies in the world (the U.S.S.R. in Afghanistan, the U.S. in Somalia, Russia in Chechnya, and the Zionist entity in southern Lebanon) and in various arenas (mountains, deserts, hills, cities).

In Afghanistan, the Mujahideen triumphed over the world's second most qualitative power at the time...Similarly, a single Somali tribe humiliated America and compelled it to remove its forces from Somalia. A short time later, the Chechen Mujahideen humiliated and defeated the Russian bear. After that, the Lebanese resistance [Hezbollah] expelled the Zionist army from southern Lebanon...

The Mujahideen proved their superiority in fourth-generation warfare using only light weaponry. They are part of the people and hide amongst the multitudes.

Abu Ubayd al-Qurashi, January/February 2002.

The last century was the century of direct colonialism in the Muslim countries...By the end of the colonialist era, the colonialist states were no longer capable of withstanding the painful blows they were taking from the hands of the Mujahideen...At this point, Zionism intervened, [suggesting] that they would protect the colonialists' interests and rescue them from the complicated situation in which they found themselves. It concealed colonialism in the most naïve way...It did not change the schemes of colonialism, rather the figures leading it.

Al Qaeda in Saudi Arabia, 3 September 2003.

Afterwards [Afghanistan], I joined the brothers in Algeria. I was in the supply team and our mission was to transfer weapons and equipment from Europe to Morocco and from there to Algeria. I remained there for months, until most of the members of that squad were imprisoned, and six of them were killed...Afterwards I participated in [jihad] in Bosnia-

Herzegovina…[and from there] I continued on to Yemen, and from Yemen to Somalia and Ogadin, a region of the Somali land occupied by the Ethiopian Crusader state that is acting to convert the Somali Muslims to Christianity…I joined my brothers in the Somali Islamic Union, and there was a lengthy affair that ended in my imprisonment for a period of two years and seven months, at the end of which I was extradited to the tyrants in the Land of the Two Holy Mosques and was jailed for a time. A month after my release, I traveled to Afghanistan and participated together with the brothers in training and fighting against the Americans. Today…I am [in Saudi Arabia] at the front.

Abu Hajjer, October 2003.

Covert and open Islamic groups have been trying for decades to establish the Islamic state, and so far they have made no progress, not even a single step, in this area. [This], while jihad for the sake of Allah has managed to establish blessed states and entities that defended the Muslims and succeeded in applying Shari'a for certain periods. The state of Sheikh Muhammad bin Abd al-Wahhab [Saudi Arabia] arose only by jihad. The state of the Taliban in Afghanistan arose only by jihad. The Islamic state in Chechnya arose only by jihad. It is true that these attempts were not perfect and did not fill the full role required, but incremental progress is a known universal principle. Yesterday, we did not dream of a state; today we establish states and they fall. Tomorrow, Allah willing, a state will arise and will not fall.

Abu Abdallah al-Sa'di, 20 January 2004.

HOSTAGES

It is permitted to strike the nonbeliever who has no covenant until he reveals the news, information and secrets of his people. The religious scholars have also permitted the killing of a hostage if he insists on withholding information from Muslims. They have permitted his killing so that he would not inform his people of what he learned about the Muslim condition, number and secrets...The scholars have also permitted the exchange of hostages for money, services, and expertise, as well as secrets of the enemy's army, plans and numbers.

Al Qaeda, 10 May 2000.

This worm [Paul Johnson] had been working for 10 years serving the Crusaders' military forces in the Land of the Two Holy Mosques, participating directly in the war against Muslims...The Mujahideen declared they would kill the hostage within 72 hours unless the Saudi government released all the Muslim prisoners in its custody. The ignorant Saudi government declared...it would not accept the Mujahideen's demands...Upon the expiration of the time period given, the Mujahideen implemented their promise and killed the hostage.

Abdul Aziz al-Muqrin, 19 June 2004.

We must therefore set up an association whose purpose is to ensure the communication of our demands to people, even if this should expose them to dangers akin to the perils of combat...such as the taking of a hostage. After raising the hullabaloo concerning him we demand that media correspondents publish our demands in full in return for his release...Our demand might be a statement or warning or justification for an operation.

Abu Bakr Naji, 2 March 2005.

HUMAN RIGHTS

The people of Islam have awakened and realized that they are the main target for the aggression of the Zionist-Crusaders' alliance. All false claims and propaganda about 'Human Rights' have been hammered down and exposed by the massacres that have taken place against Muslims in every part of the world.

Osama bin Laden, 23 August 1996.

You [the U.S.] have claimed to be the vanguards of human rights, and your Ministry of Foreign Affairs issues annual reports containing statistics of those countries that violate any human rights. However, all these things vanished when the Mujahideen hit you, and you then implemented the methods of the same documented governments that you used to curse. In America, you captured thousands of Muslims and Arabs, took them into custody without reason, court trial, or even disclosing their names. You issued newer, harsher laws.

Al Qaeda, 24 November 2002.

The human rights they [current regimes] are advocating are the rights of the criminal to the humiliation of the Muslim...The true reform begins from within us. It begins by planting the will of resistance in our hearts and in the hearts of our children and coming generations.

Ayman al-Zawahiri, 11 June 2004

INDIA

I have come here because this is my duty to tell you that Muslims should not rest in peace until we have destroyed America and India.

Masood Azhar, 5 January 2000.

The jihad is not about Kashmir only. It encompasses all of India, including Juangarh, Mavadar, and Hyderabad, etc... Today, I announce the break-up of India, insha-Allah. We will not rest until the whole of India is dissolved into Pakistan.

Hafiz Muhammad Saeed, 26 January 2000.

The effective Israeli-Indian co-operation in the security, military, and other fields is no secret to anyone. The visit by the criminal Jew [Israeli Prime Minister Ariel] Sharon—the killer of thousands of Muslims and the one who encroached on the sanctity of the al-Aqsa Mosque—to India, as well as the agreements and deals he concluded with the Indians, are only the tip of the iceberg...This U.S.-Jewish-Indian alliance is against Muslims.

Ayman al-Zawahiri, 28 September 2003.

INDONESIA

Let us examine the stand of the West and the United Nations in the developments in Indonesia when they moved to divide the largest country in the Islamic world in terms of population. This criminal, Kofi Anan [Secretary General of the U.N.], was speaking publicly and putting pressure on the Indonesian government, telling it: You have 24 hours to divide and separate East Timor from Indonesia. Otherwise, we will be forced to send in military forces to separate it by force. The Crusader Australian forces were on Indonesian shores, and in fact they landed to separate East Timor, which is part of the Islamic world.

Osama bin Laden, 3 November 2001.

Under the same cover [the United Nations] it [the United States] tore apart Indonesia and deported the Muslims of Timor to the Moluccas Islands and Poso.

Al Qaeda, 24 April 2002.

The campaigns in Indonesia are a conscious and natural response to the situation of oppression in which the nation in Palestine and Afghanistan is situated. And the daily threat against Iraq by the 'unfortunate world triangle': the Jews, the Americans and the British.

Salim al-Makhi, "Mending the Hearts of the Believers." October/November 2002.

INFIDELS

I would also like to add that our work targets world infidels in the first place. Our enemy is the Crusader alliance led by America, Britain and Israel. It is a Crusader-Jewish alliance. However, some regimes in the Arab and Muslim worlds have joined that alliance, preventing us Muslims from defending the holy Ka'ba. Our hostility is in the first place, and to the greatest extent, leveled against these world infidels, and by necessity the regimes which have turned themselves into tools for this occupation of the greatest House in the Universe and the first House of Worship [the Ka'ba] appointed for men.

Osama bin Laden, 22 December 1998.

If Muslims ally with the infidel, helping them by supplying them weapons or praising them, formulating or signing contracts with them or allowing them to assist in the military action of killing Muslims in any way, the Muslims so involved would become apostates...1). He/She has no sanctity for his life, and he must therefore be killed whether he asks for repentance or not. 2). Any marriage with a wife will become invalid, his children will no longer belong to him, and all his blood relations must be cut. 3). His money becomes permissible...or it will be taken as booty by the Mujahideen. He will receive no inheritance, nor will he pass any inheritance to others. 4). His body will not be buried with the Muslims. 5). He will be treated with animosity by all Muslims...No Muslim sister will be allowed to marry him...Anyone who gives his daughter to him will also become an apostate. 6). There is no distinction between a man or woman with respect to this...Therefore we ask Muslims with the capability, especially the army of Muslim countries to move quickly and to capture those apostates and criminals involved in these crimes, especially the ruler of Pakistan, King Fahd of Saudi Arabia and Rabbani of Afghanistan and his followers.

Fatwa on General Pervez Musharraf and the U.S.A., 16 September 2001.

Almighty Allah...is helping the believers and the Muslims. Allah says he will never be satisfied with the infidels. In terms of worldly affairs, America is strong. Even if it were twice as strong or twice that, it could not be strong enough to defeat us. We are confident that no one can harm us if Allah is with us.

Mullah Omar, 21 September 2001.

He who claims there will be a lasting peace between us and the Jews is an infidel.

Osama bin Laden, 21 October 2001.

Allah made annihilating the infidels one of his steadfast decrees...When we say that annihilating the infidel forces is a divine decree, it means that it is an immutable, valid law and a constant principle that does not change with time, place, people and circumstances...It is worthy to note that this annihilation will come either by means of a rapid and one-time collapse following a crushing blow...or by means of a gradual fall.

Sayf al-Ansari, 10 August 2002.

Monotheism and its obligations are prior to all other obligations, relations, or languages...But the infidel is an infidel whether he is an Arab or a non-Arab. He must be seen as an enemy. Furthermore, this is one of the fundamental principles of monotheism and one of the foundations of Islam.

Abd al-Rahman ibn Salem al-Shamari, August/September 2004.

INTERNATIONAL LAW

You [the Americans] are the last ones to respect the resolutions and policies of International Law, yet you claim to want to selectively punish anyone else who does the same. Israel has for more than 50 years been pushing U.N. resolutions and rules against the wall with the full support of America.

Al Qaeda, 24 November 2002.

INTERNET

Every time you [the U.S.] close a website you only further expose yourself to the world and the truth about the democracy you brag about. It is a democracy that is tailored to your measurements only. And when people oppose you, your democracy turns into the ugliest forms of domination, tyranny and despotism on earth.

Center for Islamic Studies and Research, 3 October 2002.

You might ask: What can we do when we are far from the fields of jihad? We say to you that you are in the midst of these fields...You know their positions, movements, and capabilities. You know their military soft spots and weaknesses. With this knowledge you can be a source of strength to us. This advantage will give you a decisive role, Allah willing, in serving the religion of your Lord and serving your nation...

Pass [to us] reports about important economic and military targets...of the American infidel Crusaders...You can post these reports through these sites openly. It would be better

if they were supported by photographs, or if the location is pinpointed on a scanned commercial map and attached to the report...you will be achieving one of two good things: victory or martyrdom. You know very well how to hurt the infidels most, because you know them and know their weak points.
Al Qaeda, 19 November 2002.

For using the Internet, you must go to an Internet café... never visit a site that can reveal your identity, such as those belonging to FBI, Al Qaeda or the Mujahideen...when opening an e-mail account, go to an Internet café, never do it at home... never use the same Internet café again and again...before leaving the café, remove all evidence, never leave any trace... while sending an e-mail, never use the language that could reveal your ideological commitment...Write your message in a word processor, compose, cut, paste and send. And then disconnect. Never let your e-mail open to write a message.

Al Qaeda, January 2004.

To meet our responsibility in informing the Muslim community, we declare to the whole world that we have our special media channels that we transmit information through designated websites. In our statements, we claim full responsibility for the operations we carry out against the Americans and their collaborators in the army and the police forces. We also like to make clear that we claim no responsibility for other operations and for those that do not directly receive these statements made through our regular channels.

Al Qaeda in Iraq, 13 May 2005.

IRAQ

When 60 Jews are killed inside Palestine, all the world gathers within seven days to criticize this action, while the deaths of 600,000 Iraqi children did not receive the same reaction. Killing those Iraqi children is a Crusade against Islam. We, as Muslims, do not like the Iraqi regime, but we think that the Iraqi people and their children are our brothers, and we care about their future.

Osama bin Laden, 6 December 1996.

Despite the great devastation inflicted on the Iraqi people by the Crusader-Zionist alliance, and despite the huge number of those killed, in excess of one million...despite all this, the Americans are once again trying to repeat the horrific massacres, as though they are not content with the protracted blockade imposed after the ferocious war or the fragmentation and devastation. So now they come to annihilate what is left of this people and to humiliate their Muslim neighbors.

World Islamic Front for Jihad against the Jews and Crusaders, 23 February 1998.

Look at Iraq. At one point it was given support to attack Iran when it got away from American hegemony. But when Iraq managed to acquire some strength, it is now being heavily bombarded. The people of Iraq are being crushed, while the media tries to draw attention to some aspects of the conduct of Saddam Hussein, although a few thousand Iraqi Muslims die everyday.

Osama bin Laden, 22 December 1998.

Bush the father—the ill-famed man—was the reason behind the killing of over one million children in Iraq. This is in addition to the men and women.

Osama bin Laden, 26 December 2001.

The danger of what America and its allies are preparing against Iraq and its people is not limited to overthrowing the infidel regime and a tyrant, but is aimed at killing children, women and the elderly among the Muslims, and balkanizing this great country, pillaging its wealth, and occupying a vital part of our Arab world that enables them to directly protect the Jewish occupiers and realize their [Jews'] dream in establishing their 'Greater State' from the Nile to the Euphrates...the [Muslim] people...must resist the occupiers by all means possible so that they shall feel that they are standing on a land which doesn't tolerate them, under a sky that doesn't provide them shade, and among people who are hostile towards them and who hate them.

Sulaiman Abu Ghaith, 7 December 2002.

IRAQ WAR (2003—NOW)

We are following up with great interest and extreme concern the Crusaders' preparations for war to occupy a former capital of Islam [Baghdad], loot the Muslims' wealth, and install an agent government, which would be a satellite for its masters in Washington and Tel Aviv, just like all the other treasonous and agent Arab governments. This would be in preparation for establishing the 'Greater Israel.'

Osama bin Laden, 19 January 2003.

O Mujahideen brothers in Iraq, do not be afraid of what the United States is propagating in terms of their lies about their power and their smart, laser-guided missiles. The smart bombs will have no effect worth mentioning in the hills and in the trenches, on plains, and in forests...

We also recommend luring the enemy forces into a protracted, close, and exhausting fight, using camouflaged defensive positions in plains, farms, mountains and cities. The enemy fears city and street wars most, a war in which the enemy expects grave human losses...

Regardless of the removal or the survival of the socialist party or Saddam [Hussein], Muslims in general and the Iraqis in particular must brace themselves for jihad against this unjust campaign and acquire ammunition and weapons...Under these circumstances, there will be no harm if the interests of Muslims converge with the interests of the socialists in the fight against the Crusaders, despite our belief in the infidelity of socialists.

Osama bin Laden, 19 January 2003.

Anyone who helps America, from the Iraqi hypocrites or Arab rulers...whoever...offers them bases or administrative assistance, or any kind of support or help, even if only with words, to kill Muslims in Iraq, should know that he is an apostate.

Osama bin Laden, 11 February 2003.

All of them [supporting countries] have been imposed upon you, and jihad against them is your duty. The United States has attacked Iraq, and soon it will also attack Iran, Saudi Arabia, Egypt and Sudan. The attack in Saudi Arabia and Egypt will be against the Islamic movements there.

Osama bin Laden, 8 April 2003.

The enemy [America] is now spread out, close at hand, and easy to target.

Abu Ayman al-Hilali, 17 April 2003.

After the fall of Baghdad, voices of wailing and mourning swelled in many Islamic countries, while total numbness and silence encompassed other circles...They forgot that the entire Arab world is as good as fallen, as long as Shari'a is abrogated and the people of Islam fill the prisons and detention camps...Yes, direct colonialism has returned again. Another Arab capital has fallen into its hands, as Jerusalem, Beirut and Kabul fell.

Abu Ubayd al-Qurashi, 17 April 2003.

O Iraqi people, we defeated those Crusaders several times before and expelled them out of our countries and holy shrines. You should know that you are not alone in this battle. Your Mujahid brothers are tracking your enemies and lying in wait for them. The Mujahideen in Palestine, Afghanistan, and Chechnya, and even in the heart of America and the West, are causing death to those Crusaders. The coming days will bring you the news that will heal your breasts, Allah willing.

Ayman al-Zawahiri, 21 May 2003.

To our struggling brothers in Iraq: We greet you, and we pray to Allah to be on your side in fighting the Crusaders... Allah is with you, and the entire Muslim community supports you. Rely on Allah and devour the Americans, like lions devour their prey. Bury them in the Iraqi graveyard...We thank Allah for appeasing us with the dilemma in Iraq after Afghanistan. The Americans are facing a delicate situation in both countries. If they withdraw, they will lose everything, and if they stay, they will continue to bleed to death.

Ayman al-Zawahiri, 10 September 2003.

And to the American soldiers in Iraq, I say, now that all the lies have been exposed and the greatest liar [President Bush] has been revealed, your stay on Iraq's land is compounding the oppression and is a great folly. It shows you are selling your lives for the lives of others. And you are spilling your blood to swell the bank accounts of the White House gang and their fellow arms dealers and the proprietors of great companies. And the greatest folly in life is to sell your life for the lives of others.

Osama bin Laden, 18 October 2003.

My congratulations to you [Iraqis] on your blessed efforts and jihad. You have indeed slaughtered the enemy and have pleased the hearts of all Muslims, particularly the Palestinian people...Thank you for your jihad...Be glad of the good news: America is mired in the swamps of the Tigris and Euphrates. Bush is, through Iraq and its oil, easy prey. Here is he now...in an embarrassing situation, and here is America today being ruined before the eyes of the whole world...Be aware that this war is a new Crusade against the Islamic world. It is a decisive war for the whole community.

Osama bin Laden, 18 October 2003.

I am calling upon Muslims in general and Iraqi people in particular to tell them to avoid supporting the American Crusaders and those who back them. Those who assist them, whatever they are called, are renegades and infidels. This applies to those who support parties of infidels such as the Baath party, the Kurdish parties and the like. It is also obvious that any government set up by America will be a puppet and traitorous regime.

Osama bin Laden, 18 October 2003.

Regarding the situation in Iraq and the guerrilla war... it is essential that the jihad groups there [in Iraq] unite and not separate, and that they have the political dimension to assemble the Sunnis, including the Kurds, the Arabs, and the Turkomens. All must be united under the same political power.

Sheikh Abu Omar al-Sayf, 31 December 2003.

The resistance of the Iraqi people against the occupying armies to liberate their lands and restore their national sovereignty is mandatory on each and every able Iraqi living inside and outside the country as long as he is part of the Muslim community...It is not permissible for any Muslim to provide support to the occupiers.

International Association of Muslim Scholars, 19 November 2004.

The whole world is watching this and the two adversaries: the Muslim community, on the one hand, and the

United States and its allies on the other. It is either victory and glory or misery and humiliation. The Muslim community today has a very rare opportunity to come out of subservience and enslavement to the West, and to smash the chains with which the Crusaders have fettered it.

Osama bin Laden, 27 December 2004.

The Iraqi who is waging jihad against the infidel Americans or Allawi's renegade government is our brother and companion, even if he is of Persian, Kurdish, or Turkomen origin. The Iraqi who joins this renegade government to fight against the Mujahideen, who resist occupation, is considered a

renegade and one of the infidels.

Osama bin Laden, 27 December 2004.

The Crusader propaganda apparatus continues to lie and deny. They deny the shooting down of their helicopters, well, our videos are on the way, and when the videos are shown to the entire world, the American military commanders ought to be compelled to explain their lies.

Abu Abdul Rahman al-Iraqi, 11 May 2005.

IRAQI ELECTIONS (2005)

This concept [democracy] is denying Allah the Almighty, attributing [to other deities] partnership with the Lord of heaven and earth, and [it] contradicts monotheism, the Muslims' religion. According to democracy, if the majority of the public votes in favor of a given law...then this law becomes legislation which obligates everyone, even if it contradicts Allah's religion and His law...Appealing to laws which were established by men and which contradict Allah's law is polytheism and the diversion of worship to one other than Allah...This issue [Iraqi elections], then, is a farce which [our] enemies have created in order to grant what they call legitimacy to the new government, which serves the Crusaders and carries out their designs...At the same time as the jihad groups are ardent about the people's interests...they call upon all Muslims zealous for their religion not to participate in this act of heresy, whose aim is to permit heresy and to permit behaving according to the heretical laws drawn up by the Crusaders, and to remove the great religion from the reality of our lives and to propose secularism as a substitute for it.

Army of the Supporters of the Sunna, the Jihad Warriors Army and the Islamic Army in Iraq, 30 December 2004.

If you have a nearest and dearest...for whom you are afraid, and if you do not wish to see their corpse on the 30th January roasting on piles of filthy election papers, give them this warning...let him not cast himself into a perdition that will follow him in this world and the next...let him not think that the soldiers of infidelity and apostasy can protect him.

Islamic Army in Iraq, 16 January 2005.

Now they [Americans and their Shi'ite allies] are completely preoccupied with making the big American lie called 'democracy' successful...Americans have been playing with the minds of many peoples with the lie of 'civilized democracy'; they have deluded them that their happiness and prosperity is conditional upon this inadequate human system, and subsequently the infidel American administration declared war on Iraq and Afghanistan because it is the primary protector and guardian of democracy in the world...The matter, then, is a matter of principle; it is non-negotiable, and there can be no concession regarding it whatsoever...It is a matter relating to the principles of our creed—nay, it is the very essence of our creed.

Abu Mus'ab al-Zarqawi, 23 January 2005.

Your brothers in the military wing of the Al Qaeda Organization in Iraq announce:

1. Oh enemies of Islam, prepare yourselves and fortify whatever you like, wear as much armor as you can. We have men who love death as you love life. Our fallen [go to] heaven, and yours—to hell. While your reinforcements come from the Jews and the Christians, our reinforcements come from the Blessed and Lofty Allah.

2. Take care not to go near the centers of heresy and abomination, that is, the election [booths]. He who has warned has carried out his duty; [if something happens] do not blame us, but yourselves.

3. Oh the gardens [of Eden], prepare yourselves; oh black-eyed [virgins], approach; oh brigade of martyrs, say, 'There is no God but Allah,' and 'God is the Greatest.' The martyrs' wedding is at hand.

Al Qaeda in Iraq, 26 January 2005.

ISLAM

This is an invitation that we extend to all the nations to embrace Islam, the religion that calls for justice, mercy and fraternity among all nations, not differentiating between black and white or between red and yellow, except with respect to their devotedness. All people who worship Allah, not each other, are equal before Him. We are entrusted to spread this message and to extend that call to all the people. We, nonetheless, fight against their governments and all those who approve of the injustice they practice against us. We fight the governments that are bent on attacking our religion and on stealing our wealth.

Osama bin Laden, 28 May 1998.

Allah ordered us in this religion to purify Muslim land of all non-believers, and especially the Arabian Peninsula where the Ka'ba is.

Osama bin Laden, 28 May 1998.

Jihad is a part of our religion and our Shari'a. Those who love Allah and his Prophet and this religion may not deny a part of that religion. This is a very serious matter. Whoever denies even a very minor tenet of religion would have committed the gravest sin in Islam. Such persons must renew their faith and rededicate themselves to their religion.

Osama bin Laden, 22 December 1998.

Every Muslim who sees discrimination begins to hate the Americans, the Jews and Christians. This is part of our religion and faith.

Osama bin Laden, 10 June 1999.

You should know that seeking to kill Americans and Jews everywhere in the world is one of the greatest duties [for Muslims], and the good deed most preferred by Allah, the Exalted.

Osama bin Laden, 11 February 2003.

We sacrifice our blood for our religion. Our religion is the religion of peace, of submission to Allah, the one and only, but at the same time it is the religion of might and power. We have not submitted, and we will not submit to anyone who attacks us. If we are attacked or if any Muslim is attacked in the East or the West, we will respond in kind to the one who attacked us, measure for measure.

Muhammad bin Abd al-Wahhab al-Maqit, 17 October 2003.

ISLAMIC WORLD

It is obvious that their [Americans and Zionists] zeal to have a military presence in the region and their attempt to control all the alleys and doors and charitable organizations in order to protect the regimes which are loyal to them. They are attacking any Islamic activity which represents a threat to them through bases which enable them to move quickly at any occurrence outside their calculations.

Abu-Yasir Rifa'i Ahmad Taha, April-May 1997.

It is not true that Afghanistan is being pressured because of the presence of Osama bin Laden. The whole Islamic world is being pressured. There is a design aimed at re-dividing the Muslim world, similar to what happened in Afghanistan when it was divided into five mini-states...

There is also a plan to divide Iraq into three—one in the north for Muslim Kurds, a state in the middle, and a third in the south. The same applies to the Land of the Two Holy Mosques where there is a plan to divide it into a state for the Two Mosques, another state for oil in the eastern region, and a state in the middle. This would make the people of the Two Mosques always busy trying to earn a living, and would leave a few people in the oil region who can be easily controlled.

This is a world design, and Muslims should not focus on side effects. They should unify their ranks to be able to resist this occupation.

Osama bin Laden, 22 December 1998.

There is no Muslim land today which constitutes an Islamic State. Many lands belong to Muslims and the people are Muslims, but infidelity dominates the law and order in all Muslim countries.

Fatwa on General Pervez Musharraf and the U.S.A., 16 September 2001.

American repression and imperialism is a challenge for the entire Muslim world...[linking Osama bin Laden with 9/11] is part of the U.S.'s sinister plans to strike against Afghanistan.

Jaish-e-Muhammad, Harkat-ul-Mujahideen, Al Badr and Jamiat-ul-Mujahideen, 19 September 2001.

Those who follow the movement of the criminal gang at the White House, the agents of the Jews, are preparing to attack and partition the Islamic world.

Osama bin Laden, 6 October 2002.

We also stress to honest Muslims that they should move, incite, and mobilize the Muslim community, amid such grave events and hot atmosphere, so as to liberate themselves from the unjust and renegade ruling [Muslim] regimes, which are enslaved by the United States.

Osama bin Laden, 11 February 2003.

The Muslim countries are today subject to overt or covert colonialism...A 'Karzai' [President of Afghanistan] regime exists officially in all the Muslim countries...The real ruler is Crusader America...The Americans and the agent governments that support them, like the Karzai government in Afghanistan, the [Pervez] Musharraf government in Pakistan, the [King] Fahd government in the Land of the Two Holy Mosques, and the Ali Abdallah Saleh government in Yemen, are permissible targets for the Mujahideen, according to the Shari'a...They and the Americans are identical, both in their war on [Islam] and in the extent to which they are a target for the Mujahideen.

Al Qaeda in Saudi Arabia, 3 September 2003.

The governments and regimes ruling the Muslim countries today are nothing more than examples of clear and overt collaboration with the enemies of the religion of Allah in order to remove the Shari'a of Allah from the Muslims. These governments have based their regimes and their laws on dissociation from all the values and principles of Shari'a.

Muhammad bin Shazzaf al-Shahri, 17 October 2003.

The rulers of the Muslim lands today are a gang of apostates [and] criminals, the most evil creatures created on the face of the earth, whose crimes are known to all, and they are a paradigm of treachery, deceit, misleading and repression. How many commitments have they given their people, only to then fill their graveyards and prisons with them? They have replaced Shari'a law, and they rule Muslims with the laws of Europe and America. They have shed blood and violated the religious prohibitions. They have wasted the property of the Muslims on forbidden things. All that interested them was their bellies and their enslavement to the West. They are not [protected] by any pact. Anyone who wants a lesson [on the results] of dialogue with the apostates, let them learn the lesson of the Muslim Brotherhood in Egypt, the lesson of the Islamic Front of Salvation in Algeria...and so on.

Nabil Sahraoui, 9 January 2004.

The apostate and atheist regimes in the Muslims countries are...the 'Jews of the Arabs.' They represent shocking examples of lewdness, evil, and dedication to serving the enemies of Islam...Today, America is not only concerned with these apostate regimes, but it has also conscripted them.

Abu Omar Abdul Bir, 31 January 2005.

ISRAEL

If the Americans' aims behind these wars are religious and economic, the aim is also to serve the Jews' petty state and divert attention from its occupation of Jerusalem and murder of Muslims there. The best proof of this is their eagerness to destroy Iraq, the strongest neighboring Arab state, and their endeavor to fragment all the states of the region—such as Iraq, Saudi Arabia, Egypt and Sudan—into paper statelets, and through their disunion and weakness to guarantee Israel's survival and the continuation of the brutal Crusader occupation of the Peninsula.

World Islamic Front for Jihad against the Jews and Crusaders, 23 February 1998.

We swore that America wouldn't live in security until we live it truly in Palestine. This showed the reality of America, which puts Israel's interest above it own people's interest. America won't get out of this crisis until it gets out of the Arabian Peninsula and until it stops its support of Israel. This equation can be understood by any American child, but Bush, because he's an Israeli agent, cannot understand this equation unless the swords threaten him above his head.

Osama bin Laden, 21 October 2001.

The [U.S.] government will take the American people and the West in general will enter into a choking life, into an unsupportable hell, because of the fact that those governments have very strong ties, and are on the payroll of the Zionist lobby, which serves the needs of Israel, who kills our sons and children without right so they can keep on ruling with total control.

Osama bin Laden, 23 May 2002.

The close link between America and the Zionist entity is in itself a curse for America. In addition to the high cost incurred by the U.S. Treasury as a result of this alliance, the strategic cost is also exorbitant because this close link has turned the attack against America into an attack against the Zionist entity and vice versa. This contributes to bringing the Muslim community together and pushing it strongly to rally around the jihad experience.

Al-Ansar, 12 June 2002.

The creation and continuation of Israel is one of the greatest crimes, and you [America] are the leader of its criminals. And of course there is no need to explain and prove the degree of American support for Israel. The creation of Israel is a crime which must be erased. Each and every person whose hands have become polluted in the contribution towards this crime must pay its price and pay for it heavily.

Al Qaeda, 24 November 2002.

ITALY

We have started with the warning to the Italian government and its cruel leaders [Prime Minister] Berlusconi...and his submission to the rule of America. Wait for us Berlusconi... we will start with you, O' Berlusconi, and we will make the blood flow until you return to the correct path...remove your murderous forces from Iraq.

Abu Hafs al-Masri Brigades, 28 July 2004.

We in the Jihad Organization in Iraq announce that Allah's verdict has been executed on the two Italian prisoners by slaughtering them, after the Italian government headed by the evil Berlusconi ignored our sole condition to withdraw from Iraq. We in the Jihad Organization warn the Italian government that we will continue to strike...We will make Iraq a cemetery for you.

Al-Jihad Organization in Iraq, 22 September 2004.

We tell the Italian Cross worshippers that we vow never to stop fighting you [Italians], and we ask Allah to help us in striking your necks.

Al Qaeda in Iraq, 16 March 2005.

JEWS

The enmity between us and the Jews goes far back in time and is deep rooted. There is no question that war between the two of us is inevitable.

Osama bin Laden, 28 May 1998.

The American government is throwing away the lives of Americans in Saudi Arabia for the interests of the Jews. The Jews are a people who Allah cited in his holy book, the *Qur'an*, as those who attacked prophets with lies and killings, and attacked Mary and accused her of a great sin. They are a people who killed Allah's prophets—would they not kill, rape and steal from humans? They believe that all humans are created for their use, and found that the Americans are the best-created beings for that use.

Osama bin Laden, 28 May 1998.

I have already said that we are not hostile to the United States. We are against the [U.S. government] system, which makes other nations slaves of the United States, or forces them to mortgage their political and economic freedom. This system is totally in the control of the American Jews, whose first priority is Israel, not the United States. It is clear that the American people are themselves the slaves of the Jews and are forced to live according to the principles and laws laid down by them. So the punishment should reach Israel. In fact, it is Israel which is giving a blood bath to innocent Muslims, and the U.S. is not uttering a single word.

Osama bin Laden, 28 September 2001.

We are in a decisive battle with the Jews and those who support them from the Crusaders and the Zionists. We won't hesitate to kill the Israelis who occupied our land and kill our children and women day and night. And every person who will side with them should blame themselves only.
Osama bin Laden, 21 October 2001.

The Jewish lobby has taken America and the West hostage.

Osama bin Laden, 7 November 2001.

In every country, we should hit their [Jews] organizations, institutions, clubs and hospitals. The targets must be identified, carefully chosen and include their largest gatherings so that any strike should cause thousands of deaths.

Manual of Afghan Jihad, 2 February 2002.

The Jews have lied about the Creator, and even more so about His creations. The Jews are the murderers of the prophets, the violators of agreements...These are the Jews: usurers and whoremongers. They will leave you nothing, neither this world nor religion.

Osama bin Laden, 11 February 2003.

The Jewish Threat: This threat has two aspects: The first is a Jewish plan, based on religious motives, to control Iraq. The second has to do with ending the Iraqi threat to Israel's existence.

Al Qaeda, 25 April 2003.

The breast of the Jews—Allah's curses be upon them— are filled with an arrogance that is not present in others, and therefore they have not settled for the kind of covert colonialism that satisfied the Crusader countries. Likewise, their occupation of Muslim Palestine stems from the belief that they cannot give it up, or else they would be apostates from their Judaism...The issue of Palestine is the issue of the Islamic world...but the Zionist media and the collaborating media neutralized the non-Arab Muslims by calling it 'the Arab issue.'

Al Qaeda in Saudi Arabia, 3 September 2003.

JIHAD

Jihad is the highest peak of Islam. Jihad is the most excellent form of worship, and by means of it the Muslim can reach the highest of ranks...It [jihad] will be like the small spark which ignites a large keg of explosives, for the Islamic movement brings about an eruption of the hidden capabilities of the Muslim community, and a gushing forth of the springs of Good stored up in its depth...The obligation of jihad today remains individually obligatory until the liberation of the last piece of land which was in the hands of Muslims but has been occupied by the Disbelievers.

Abdullah Azzam, 15 April 1987.

All these crimes and sins committed by the Americans are a clear declaration of war on Allah, His Messenger [Muhammad], and Muslims. And Islamic clerics have throughout Islamic history unanimously agreed that jihad is an individual duty if the enemy destroys the Muslim countries...The ruling to kill the Americans and their allies—civilians and military—is an individual duty for every Muslim who can do it in any country in which it is possible to do it, in order to liberate the al-Aqsa Mosque and the Holy Mosque [in Mecca] from their grip, and in order for their armies to move out of all the lands of Islam, defeated and unable to threaten any Muslim.

World Islamic Front for Jihad against the Jews and Crusaders, 23 February 1998.

Nowadays, jihad needs to be waged by the Muslim community. The obligation to engage in jihad may be dropped if people suffer from disability.

Osama bin Laden, 10 June 1999.

The people who had the honor of engaging in jihad in Afghanistan, Bosnia-Herzegovina, or Chechnya—we had such an honor- are certain that the Muslim community nowadays can, Allah willing, engage in jihad against the enemies of Islam, particularly, the external archenemy, the Crusader-Jewish alliance.

Osama bin Laden, 10 June 1999.

The Americans wanted to fight the Russians with Muslim blood, and they could only justify that [to the Muslims] by triggering the word jihad. Unfortunately for everyone except the Muslims, when the button of jihad is pushed, it does not come back that easy. It keeps going on and on until the Muslim empire swallows every existing empire.

Abu Hamza, 27 September 2001.

Jihad is the sixth undeclared pillar of Islam...Al Qaeda wants to keep jihad alive and active, and make it a part of the daily life of the Muslims. It wants to give it the status of worship...We are in favor of armed jihad only against those infidel governments which are killing innocent Muslim men, women and children just because they are Muslims.

Osama bin Laden, 28 September 2001.

Jihad is a duty to liberate the al-Aqsa Mosque, and to help the powerless in Palestine, Iraq, Lebanon and in every Muslim country. There is no doubt that the liberation of the Arabian Peninsula from infidels is a duty as well.

Osama bin Laden, 21 October 2001.

O Muslims of the World, the question now is no longer if the attacks on America [9/11 attacks] were correct or not, for what happened, happened; supports it the one who supports it, and opposes it the one who opposes it. The question now is what is the obligation of the Muslim community towards this new Crusade against Afghanistan?

What is the ruling on the one who allies with the Crusaders and stands by their side in any manner? That which this Muslim community has agreed upon, and that which the scholars have agreed upon is that in this condition in which we are in today, jihad against the invaders becomes a personal obligation upon every Muslim.

Mullah Omar, 2 November 2001.

We are carrying on the mission of our Prophet Muhammad...The mission is to spread the word of Allah, not to indulge massacring people. We ourselves are the target of killings, destruction and atrocities. We are only defending ourselves. This is defensive jihad. We want to defend our people and our land. That is why I say that if we don't get security, the Americans, too, will not get security. This is a simple formula that even an American child can understand. This is the formula of live and let live.

Osama bin Laden, 7 November 2001.

Jihad has become obligatory upon each and every Muslim...The time has come when all the Muslims of the world, especially the youth, should unite and...continue jihad till these forces are crushed to naught, all the anti-Islamic forces are wiped off the face of this Earth, and Islam takes over the whole world and all the other false religions.

Osama bin Laden, 9 December 2001.

[Jihad] is an unavoidable issue for the Muslim community when it moves seriously to establish this [Islamic] state. This state, without whose establishment the religion of Islam as revealed cannot be established, is the realization of the empowerment that Allah has promised to his believing friends.

Sayf al-Ansari, 28 January 2002.

But the question is how the torments [against infidels] that Allah wants carried out by our hands will be implemented... The torments certainly will not be carried out by means of preaching...[but] by means of jihad will Allah torment them.

Sayf al-Ansari, 24 August 2002.

The most important religious duty—after belief itself—is to ward off and fight the enemy aggressor...Jihad is obligatory now for the Muslim community, which is in a state of sin unless it gives of its sons, its possessions, and its powers, whatever is required, to maintain jihad, which will preserve all Muslims in Palestine and elsewhere from the military might of the infidels...Today personal participation in jihad, though it is incumbent on the Muslim community as a whole, is especially emphasized where young men are concerned, rather than with regard to the middle-aged and elderly. Likewise, the obligation to participate financially in jihad is emphasized primarily with regard to the wealthy...It is incumbent upon the Muslim community to help them, encourage them, and facilitate things for them, so that they can defend it [Muslim community] and protect it from injustice, shame and sin.

Osama bin Laden, 11 February 2003.

Even if people disagree today regarding which of these two groups—the apostate traitor agents [the Arab governments] or the colonialist enemies [the Americans]—is more worthy to wage jihad against, there need be no disagreement that jihad is the solution for dealing with both of them.

Al Qaeda in Saudi Arabia, 3 September 2003.

A tremendous obligation has been entrusted upon us—jihad for the sake of Allah...Allah has imposed the obligation of jihad in [several] cases, all of which exist in this generation: starting from repelling the aggression of the infidels, through fighting the apostates, supporting the oppressed, and liberating captives and prisoners.

Sulaiman al-Dosari, *The Voice of Jihad*, no. 1, October 2003.

My jihad-fighting brother, don't you want Paradise? Don't you want to protect yourself from Hell?...Kill the polytheist... kill the one whom Allah ordered you to kill and whom the Prophet of Allah [Muhammad] incited you against.

Sheikh Nasser al-Najdi, October 2003.

Explosions are an integral part of jihad. "This is the element that shook the armies of the Cross, and turned the life of the Jews into hell." And he asks "Are the suicide operations merely explosions?" And he concludes: "Why should we be surprised? Our times require such amazement. If people are too afraid to respond to the call for jihad, what should they do when their scholars are planting in them the seeds of disgrace and irrigate them with humiliation and collapse. They cover it with disguise of wisdom and tranquility...telling them 'explosion' is not the way for reform."

Abu Abdallah al-Sa'di, October 2003.

Brothers in Islam, jihad is one of the commandments of Islam and a solid pillar of this religion...jihad, which has earned the label of 'the peak of Islam,' is the sign of the glory and grace of Islam and of the Muslims, and no Muslim doubts that jihad for the sake of Allah is one of the greatest commandments of our religion, a commandment that has preserved the existence, the glory, and the honor of the Muslim community. Similarly, it is no secret to any intelligent Muslims that one of the reasons for the defeat of the Muslim community and its loss today is the disappearance of the banner of jihad for the sake of Allah.

Muhammad bin Shazzaf al-Shahri, 17 October 2003.

Preparing [for jihad] is a personal commandment that applies to every Muslim even when jihad [itself] is a commandment applying [only] to all Muslims as a community, and all the more so at this time, when [jihad] has become also a commandment applying to every Muslim personally with the aim of repelling the aggressive enemy who has invaded the Muslim land.

Because many of Islam's young people do not yet know how to bear arms, not mention use them, and because the agents of the Cross are hobbling the Muslims and preventing them from planning [jihad] for the sake of Allah—your brothers the Mujahideen in the Arabian peninsula have decided to publish this booklet to serve the Mujahid brother in his place of isolation, and he will do the exercises and act according to the military knowledge included within it...

JIHAD

These are times of jihad and preparation for jihad. In the time of the Mongol invasion, it didn't help the residents of Baghdad that most of them were clerics and educators.

Introduction, *Al-Battar*, December 2003/January 2004.

Muslims! Go out to [fight] jihad for the sake of Allah! Paradise has already flung open its gates, and the virgins of paradise are already decked out in anticipations of their grooms—this is Allah's promise. He [Allah] will not grant peace of mind to anyone who has a heart until he has gone out to fight against Allah's enemies, as he was commanded.

Sa'ud bin Hamoud al-Utaybi, October 2004.

We pray for the jihad fighters in Fallujah and in Iraq, Afghanistan, Chechnya, the Arabian Peninsula...in wounded Palestine, which the most wicked of all humans [Jews] have been flooding with iniquity for more than 50 years, without there being anyone to stop them, and in Egypt, on whose borders your valiant brothers took action and attacked a hotel in which Jews were gathered and killed dozens of them as an offering to Allah before Ramadan [Taba, Egypt bombings, 7 October 2004]. We ask of Allah that he not deny them [their] reward for this colossal feat.

Sa'ud bin Hamoud al-Utaybi, October 2004.

Men of jihad, this is your festive season since jihad, in a state of fasting, has a particularly delectable taste for the believers, especially with the dignity of the month of Ramadan. How wonderful it is to delight in the breaking of the fast and to taste the killing of infidels, to delight in the sound of the wailing of tyrants and lowly degenerates, and the voices of the condemnations on the part of evil people and their collaborators broadcast on the TV stations...condemning the death of their infidel masters and their servants.

Sheikh Aaamer bin Abdallah al-Aamer, October 2004.

The one who stays behind and fails to join the Mujahideen when jihad becomes an individual duty commits a cardinal sin...The most pressing duty after faith is repelling the aggressor enemy. This means that the Muslim community should devote its resources, sons, and money to fight the infidels and drive them out of its land.

Osama bin Laden, 27 December 2004.

I urge all of the fighting brothers everywhere to join under the flag of unity and to declare that their jihad is for the sake of getting back the last Caliphate and the Shari'a. I urge my free brothers in the Peninsula of the Prophet [Arabian Peninsula] to fight the apostates and drive them and the infidels from the Arabian Peninsula.

Abu Yasser Sayyaf, 9 January 2005.

JORDANIAN GOVERNMENT

Whoever wants a recent real-life example for the role of America in deciding to depose someone should look at the case of Prince Hassan ibn Talal of Jordan. After he had been viceroy for a number of decades, his brother Hussein returned from America a few days before his death, determined to depose his brother, and [indeed] he deposed him. He [Hassan] acquiesced, and became a mere political footnote. It is this [fate] that Prince Abdallah fears [would befall him] should he disobey his protector—America. Thus, it is no secret that those who make decisions about important things are in America.

Osama bin Laden, 27 December 2004.

The Jordanian regime is a pagan infidel regime. Nevertheless, the rulers of Riyadh were allied with King Hussein, and if a [Saudi] preacher or writer described him [Hussein] as an agent of the Jews, he would be subject to penalty on the part of the Riyadh regime, through laws that were legislated specifically for this purpose. However, when King Hussein entered an alliance with Saddam, when he [Saddam] invaded Kuwait, King Fahd washed his hands of his former ally, and the Riyadh newspapers filled up with documents and pictures proving that Hussein ibn Talal was an agent of the Jews—which was true, for he was indeed that. On the other hand, the Jordanian newspapers filled with documents and pictures proving that the rulers of Riyadh were agents of the English, and subsequently, of America, which is true, for they are indeed that.

Osama bin Laden, 27 December 2004.

KASHMIR

Today, the infidels want to keep the Muslims clenched under their control and want to abolish jihad at all costs... The Mujahideen of Laskhar-e-Taiba have continued the jihad despite all the negative propaganda against them...the issue of Kashmir can only be resolved through jihad.

Hafiz Muhammad Saeed, 26 January 2000.

The Mujahideen in Kashmir are engaged in a jihad to please Allah. We pray for them. They are part of us. All of us are like a body. If any part of the body has pain, the other parts also feel it. India's enmity toward Islam and Muslims is growing. All Muslims are obligated to undertake jihad against India and to support the forces engaged in jihad.

Osama bin Laden, 20-27 August 2000.

What is the crime of the Kashmiri people, and what are the directives that the 'servants of the cow' [Indian Hindus] lord over them, so that their blood has been shed for more than fifty years?

Al Qaeda, 24 April 2002.

Kashmir will not be solved by talks, not by American arbitration, not by its division but only by jihad, jihad, jihad!

Hafiz Muhammad Saeed, February 2003.

KUWAIT

[If U.S. forces don't leave the country] an event will occur in which many innocent victims will fall, and you will be responsible for these victims for your opposition to our demands...if you refuse, then you have chosen the perilous course, and it will be the end to your tyranny.

Peninsula Lions Brigades, 1 February 2005.

MADRID, SPAIN BOMBINGS (11 MARCH 2004)

We declare our responsibility for what happened in Madrid exactly two-and-a-half years after the attacks on New York and Washington. It is a response to your collaboration with the criminals Bush and his allies. This is a response to the crimes that you have caused in the world, and specifically in Iraq and Afghanistan, and there will be more, if Allah wills it. You love life and we love death, which gives an example of what the Prophet Muhammad said. If you don't stop your injustices, more and more blood will flow and these attacks will seem very small compared to what can occur in what you call terrorism.

Abu Dujan al-Afghani, 13 March 2004.

MARTYRDOM

Being killed for Allah's cause is a great honor achieved by only those who are the elite of the Muslim community. We love this kind of death for Allah's cause as much as you like to live. We have nothing to fear for. It is something we wish for.

Osama bin Laden, March 1997.

He [the member] has to be willing to do the work and undergo martyrdom for the purpose of achieving the goal and establishing the religion of majestic Allah on earth.

Al Qaeda, 10 May 2000.

Allah opens up ways and creates love in the hearts of people for those who walk on the path of Allah with their lives, property and children. Believe it, through jihad a man gets everything he desires. And the biggest desire of a Muslim is the life after death. Martyrdom is the shortest way of attaining an eternal life.

Osama bin Laden, 28 September 2001.

We stress the importance of the martyrdom operations against the enemy—operations that have inflicted harm on the

United States and Israel, and have been unprecedented in their history, thanks to Allah.

Osama bin Laden, 19 January 2003.

All the nations of the world will not be able to squash the spark Muhammad Atta and his hero brothers ignited in the hearts of the youngsters of the Muslim community with their blessed operation. The blood of each and every martyr meeting his Creator was also the biggest motivation that led all of those who were with him. The sweet smell of martyrdom, along with their captivating smiles, lit the fire of competition to become martyrs and be in the presence of Allah. Many times I had to ask the leaders of the groups [in Afghanistan post U.S. invasion] to restrain the fervor of the youngsters and not let them chase the enemy outside the realm of the set plan.

Saif al-Adel, March 2003.

The spirit of martyrdom is our strength and our weapon for the sake of the survival of our religion, and for resistance to any domestic or foreign attempt to distort our religion.

Osama bin Laden, July 2003.

Our military martyrdom operations will not stop, Allah willing, in order to elevate the word of Allah.

Hazem al-Kashmiri, 17 October 2003.

What we are doing today [12 May 2003, martyrdom attacks in Riyadh, Saudi Arabia] is a deed against the enemies of Allah, the Americans, and the others in the Land of the Two Holy Mosques, and it is in compliance with Allah and with the call of His Messenger [Muhammad]...It is support for our oppressed brothers everywhere. Oh Americans, wait for us. We have brought slaughter upon you...This deed is a gift to the procession of light...in which the jihad warriors and the martyrs marched, on the path they have cushioned with body parts, irrigated with blood and paved with skulls.

Muhammad bin Shazzaf al-Shahri, 17 October 2003.

At the battle of Khobar [Saudi Arabia, 29 May 2004] there was no choice but to carry out suicide operations...All took into account that none would return, and that they would fight until they were killed and [thus] realize the idea of plunging themselves into the midst of the enemy.

Fawwaz bin Muhammad al-Nashami, June 2004.

Become diligent in carrying out martyrdom operations; these operations, praise be to Allah, have become a great source of terror for the enemy...These are the most important questions.

Osama bin Laden, 27 December 2004.

The huge gap between what the enemy of Allah has [in terms of personnel, weapons, logistic support, etc.] and what they [the Mujahideen] have, led them to conclude that they must come up with an effective way to make up for their deficiency in order for the torch of jihad to stay lit. Martyrdom operations were the answer. Therefore, the Martyrdom Seekers Brigade came into existence. Graduates of this Brigade have wasted no time and have sped as fast as they can towards the enemies of Allah in order to pound their shelters, spread terror in their hearts, and win the pleasure of Allah. They have raced as far as they can on the road to paradise.

Abu Mus'ab al-Zarqawi, 18 May 2005.

MEDIA, WESTERN

The media sector is in the same category as it strives to beautify the persons of the leaders, to drowse the community, and to fulfill the plans of the enemies through keeping the people occupied with the minor matters, and to stir their emotions and desires until corruption becomes widespread amongst the believers.

Osama bin Laden, October/November 1996.

The Westerners have been under the impression that we are butchers...The Western masses have fallen under the effect of Jewish media who do not broadcast on Muslims except that we butcher, and without showing that the number of those of us who were butchered is the biggest number.

Osama bin Laden, 28 May 1998.

My word to American journalists is not to ask why we did that, but to ask what has their government done that has forced us to defend ourselves.

Osama bin Laden, 28 May 1998.

When jihad was obscured for a long time, we saw the emergence of a generation of students who did not experience the heat of jihad. They were affected by the U.S. media that invaded Islamic countries. Without even engaging in combat, they suffered a psychological defeat. They acknowledge the necessity for jihad. Nonetheless, they say that they cannot fulfill such an obligation.

Osama bin Laden, 10 June 1999.

The United States has an advantage media-wise and has great media power that varies its standards according to its needs.

Osama bin Laden, 10 June 1999.

In fact, the Western media is left with nothing else. It has no other theme [terrorism] to survive for a long time...

The Western media is unleashing such a baseless propaganda, which makes us surprised, but it reflects on what is in their hearts, and gradually they themselves become captive of this propaganda. They become afraid of it and begin to cause harm to themselves. Terror is the most dreaded weapon in the modern age, and the Western media is mercilessly using it against its own people. It can add fear and helplessness in the psyche of the people of Europe and the United States. It means that what the enemies of the United States cannot do, its media is doing. You can understand as to what will be the performance of the nation in a war which suffers from fear and helplessness.

Osama bin Laden, 28 September 2001.

The proof came when the U.S. government pressured the media not to run our statements that are not longer than a very few minutes. They felt that the truth had started to reach the American people, the truth that we are not terrorists as they understand it, but because we are being attacked in Palestine, Iraq, Lebanon, Sudan, Somalia, Kashmir, the Philippines and everywhere else...They forgot all about fair and objective reporting, and reporting the other side of the issue. I tell you freedom and human rights in America are doomed.

Osama bin Laden, 21 October 2001.

The American battle is a psychological battle that depends on the media and the magical effect of the microphone... [The Americans are] also careful to putrefy the surrounding medium of their rivals through offering generous rewards to whoever kills the so and so leader or reports him. The also stipulate the form of the succeeding regimes and nominate its individuals...Unfortunately, the Arab media is one of the tools of this psychological warfare.

Saif al-Adel, March 2003.

MEMBERS

The member of the organization must be a Muslim. How can an unbeliever, someone from a revealed religion [Christian, Jew], a secular person, a Communist, etc. protect Islam and Muslims, and defend their goals and secrets when he does not believe in that religion [Islam]?...

He [the member] has to be willing to do the work and undergo martyrdom for the purpose of achieving the goal and establishing the religion of majestic Allah on earth...

[The member] should have a calm personality that allows him to endure psychological traumas such as those involving bloodshed, murder, arrest, imprisonment, and reverse psychological traumas such as killing one or all of his organization's comrades.

Al Qaeda, 10 May 2000.

A senior member who betrays his brothers to the regime where they live should be punished in such a way that he would desire death for the rest of his days. But if a brother is killed as a result of his betrayal, then he must be killed to make an example of him.

Manual of Afghan Jihad, 2 February 2002.

Each member shall resolve his personal disputes in his personal life and should not drag the group or the leadership into his personal problems...When the leadership advises you to work with certain individuals or introduces you to some individuals, you shall never have personal friendships with them. If the leadership arranges a meeting with a responsible friend, or you come into contact with one...do not mention it to anybody...not even to those within the organization. If a responsible friend gives you a secret duty...you will not mention this job even to your closest friend within the organization, no matter how trustworthy that person may be. Similarly, if a responsible person has given you a message for another friend, this message should never be mentioned to a third friend within the organization...you will deliver this message only to the person it's meant for...you will personally deliver this message and will never use another person for this purpose.

Al Qaeda, January 2004.

MOMBASSA, KENYA ATTACK (28 NOVEMBER 2002)

Al Qaeda announces officially its responsibility for the two attacks in Mombassa. This statement comes as a challenge to the American enemy and to let it know Al Qaeda is capable of reaching any place in the world. These two operations were meant to destroy all the dreams of the Jewish-Crusader covenant of safeguarding their strategic interests in this region and prove the failure of America and its allies who amassed their huge naval fleets around the Horn of Africa to pursue the Mujahideen...[Calls on Africa's Muslims to] follow in the footsteps of the heroes of the Mombassa operations to turn the land into a hell under the feet of the Jewish and Crusader occupiers.

Political Bureau of Al Qaeda, December 2002.

I would like to reconfirm what the Political Bureau of Al Qaeda has stated concerning the two attacks in Mombassa, Kenya, against the Jewish interests and the other Mujahideen operations against the Crusader-Jewish alliance...The Jewish-Crusader alliance will not be safe anywhere from the Mujahideen attacks. We will hit the most vital installations and strategic interests with all means at our disposal.

Sulaiman Abu Ghaith, 7 December 2002.

MUJAHIDEEN

The Mujahideen...are waging an unrelenting jihad and continue to endure on this path...It would not be an understatement to say that for every Mujahid who is martyred, another handful, filled with enthusiasm for jihad, replace him.

The Mujahid is the one who not only desires to destroy the enemies of Allah but loves also to be slain in his way.

Esa al-Hindi, 1999.

The Mujahideen are a part of this blessed and victorious Muslim community. They are the vanguard that has pledged itself to spark the confrontation between our enemies and us. Thus, it is not fighting instead of the Muslim community, but it is working as an activator for the Muslim community against its enemies so that it may rise altogether to face the occupying and invading enemy.

Sulaiman Abu Ghaith, 7 December 2002.

You, the Mujahideen, there is now a rare and golden opportunity to make America bleed in Iraq, both economically and in terms of human losses and morale. Don't miss out on this opportunity, lest you regret it.

Osama bin Laden, 27 December 2004.

O you Mujahideen! You are this Muslim community's chosen few, its first line of defense, its safety valve, and its well-constructed fence. You are the vigilant, guardian rock upon which the American ignorance has crumbled to pieces. With your determination to fight the Cross worshippers and their collaborators from our own skin, not only do you defend the

Land of the Two Rivers, but you also defend the entire Muslim community.

Abu Mus'ab al-Zarqawi, 29 April 2005.

MUSLIM UNITY

If it is not possible to push back the enemy except by the collective movement of the Muslim people, then there is a duty on the Muslims to ignore the minor differences among themselves; the ill effect of ignoring these differences, at a given period of time, is much less than the ill effect of the occupation of the Muslims' land by the main infidels.

Osama bin Laden, 23 August 1996.

Muslims should cooperate with one another and should be supportive of one another, and they should promote righteousness and mercy. They should all unite in the fight against polytheism, and they should pool all their resources and their energy to fight the Americans and the Zionists and those with them. They should, however, avoid side fronts and rise over the small problems, for these are less detrimental. Their fight should be directed against unbelief and unbelievers.

Osama bin Laden, 28 May 1998.

Al Qaeda's Mujahideen have proven from the outset that they rise above the traditional [internal] conflicts.

Abu Ubayd al-Qurashi, January/February 2002.

The unity to which we are calling Muslims today does not necessarily need putting an end to disputes and their existence is not damaging.

Osama bin Laden, 14 October 2002.

MUSLIMS

We—with Allah's help—call on every Muslim who believes in Allah and wishes to be rewarded to comply with Allah's order to kill the Americans and plunder their money, wherever and whenever they find it. We also call on Muslim clerics, leaders, youths and soldiers to launch the raid on Satan's U.S. troops and the devil's supporters allying with them, and to displace those who are behind them so that they may learn a lesson.

World Islamic Front for Jihad against the Jews and Crusaders, 23 February 1998.

The leaders in America and in other countries as well have fallen victim to Jewish Zionist blackmail. They have mobilized their people against Islam and against Muslims. These are portrayed in such a manner as to drive people to rally against them. The truth is that the whole Muslim world is the victim of international terrorism, engineered by America at the United Nations. We are a nation whose sacred symbols have been looted, and whose wealth and resources have been plundered. It is normal for us to react against the forces that invade our land and occupy it.

Osama bin Laden, 28 May 1998.

We must state that all the Muslim peoples who have been annihilated by the worldwide Zionist Crusade did not commit any crime except to say, "Allah is our Lord." The Zionist-Crusader coalition does not need directives or guilty verdicts against Muslims to begin its war or to continue it. It did not stand around with its hands tied previously, waiting for excuses to launch its wars of extermination against Muslims.

Al Qaeda, 24 April 2002.

MUSLIMS, KILLING OF FELLOW

Suppose that the Americans had attacked an Islamic country and kidnapped my children, the children of Osama bin Laden, to use as a shield, and then started to kill Muslims as is the case in Lebanon, Palestine, and these days in Iraq, and also when they supported the Serbs in massacring the Muslims in Bosnia. According to Islamic jurisprudence, if we abstain from firing on the Americans lest we should kill these Muslims [used by them as shields], the harm that could befall Muslims at large, who are being attacked, outweighs the good of saving the lives of these Muslims used as a shield. This means that in a case like this, when it becomes apparent that it would be impossible to repel these Americans without assaulting them, even if this involved the killing of Muslims, this is permissible under Islam.

Osama bin Laden, 22 December 1998.

To the dogs of the country, why do you help the tyrants against your brothers? Is it for a fistful of money that you tail the Muslims and torture the Mujahideen? Cling to Allah. Stop harming us. Otherwise—and I swear by Allah, who helped my 19 brothers [9/11 hijackers] overcome the Americans in their own homes—you will encounter on our part only the sword and the head of the spear.

Muhammad bin Shazzaf al-Shahri, 17 October 2003.

It's worth noting that the Mujahideen were very careful not to spill Muslim blood. They differentiated between Muslims and the infidel Crusaders. They let Muslims go and led them away from the fighting area in contrast to the renegade government forces who were shooting indiscriminately everywhere...We thank Allah very much for this exceptional blessed operation. We renew our commitment to defeat the forces of the Cross and the oppressor, to liberate the land of the Muslims, to live under Allah's rule, to implement His orders, and purify the Arabian Peninsula from the polytheists.

Al Quds Company of Al Qaeda in the Arabian Peninsula, 30 May 2004.

We do not declare [Muslim] people collectively to be infidels and do not consider the killing of Muslims to be permissible. If some Muslims are killed during the operations of the Mujahideen, we pray for Allah's mercy upon them. This is to be considered accidental manslaughter, and we ask Allah to forgive us for it, and we bear responsibility for it.

Osama bin Laden, 27 December 2004.

Admittedly, the killing of a number of Muslims whom it is forbidden to kill is undoubtedly a great evil; however, it is permissible to commit this evil—indeed, it is even required—in order to ward off a greater evil, namely, the evil of suspending jihad...This inevitably means surrendering the land and the believers to the hands of unbelievers who bitterly hate Islam and its people.

Abu Mus'ab al-Zarqawi, 18 May 2005.

NAIROBI, KENYA AND DAR ES SALAM, TANZANIA, U.S. EMBASSIES BOMBINGS (7 AUGUST 1998)

Given the American Crusader and Jewish Israeli occupation of the environs of the al-Aqsa mosque, given what the Jews are doing in Palestine by killing our children and women and... destroying the houses of our innocent brethren,...given that more than a million Iraqis have died; given the imprisonment of Muslim clerics in America and in the countries dominated by the United States, and given the theft of Muslim fortunes through oil development, we are compelled to wage the jihad throughout the world and at all times.

Combating the United States and their allies, the Jews of Israel, is a life and death struggle. Before Nairobi, we had warned Muslims to avoid contact with everything American, and we repeat this warning.

Islamic Army for the Liberation of the Holy Places, 12 August 1998.

On Friday, we learned that two huge explosions in the capitals of Kenya and Tanzania targeted the American embassies [and succeeded] thanks to the clear plans and the determination of the militants...These two embassies that the Islamic Army for the Liberation of the Holy Places blew up had supervised the killing of thirteen thousand Somali civilians at least in the treacherous attack led by the United States against this Muslim country.

World Islamic Front for Jihad against the Jews and Crusaders, 12 August 1998.

I gave no orders [for the attacks in East Africa], but I am very happy about what happened to the Americans there... What I know is that those who risked their lives to earn the pleasure of Allah...are the real men, the true personification of the word men. They managed to rid the Muslim community of disgrace. We highly respect them and hold them in the highest esteem, and pray to Allah...to accept them as martyrs and permit them to intercede on behalf of their kin.

Osama bin Laden, 22 December 1998.

It was a painful blow. They [the Americans] had not sustained such a blow since the blowing up of the Marines in Lebanon. The Nairobi [U.S.] Embassy was actually six embassies combined in one. The brutal U.S. invasion of Somalia kicked off from there...For the past few decades plots have been hatched to partition Sudan from there. These plots are hatched in Nairobi. As is widely known, the U.S. Embassy in Nairobi is the agency that is doing this. The greatest CIA center in eastern Africa is located at that embassy. Thanks to Allah's grace to Muslims, the blow was successful and great. They deserved it. It made them taste what we tasted during the massacres committed in Sabra, Shatila, Dayr Yasin, Qana, Hebron and elsewhere.

Osama bin Laden, 10 June 1999.

NATIONALISM

Fighting should be for the sake of the one God. It should not be for championing ethnic groups, or for championing the non-Islamic regimes in all Arab countries, including Iraq.

Osama bin Laden, 19 January 2003.

The [Arab] nation states...are a Western model that the West created to allow it to build up its general colonialist plan for the Islamic East. These countries have no religious foundation, and have neither a right to exist nor a popular base. They were forced upon the Muslim peoples, and their survival is linked to the Western forces that created them. Therefore, the general aim of the jihad and the Mujahideen is to strike at the foundations and infrastructure of the Western colonialist program or at the so-called world order—or, to put it bluntly, to defeat the Crusaders in the battle that has been going on for over a century. Their defeat means, simply, the elimination of all forms of nation-states, such that all that remains is the natural existence familiar to Islam—the regional entity under the great Islamic state.

Louis Attiya Allah, December 2003.

And these are the lessons we learned: The collapse of the national identities. When these are opposed to the Shari'a or attempt to rival it, and when they cause division among people and [provide a basis for] allegiances, then these national identities should fall, and Arab nationalism first and foremost.

Abd al-Rahman ibn Salem al-Shamari, August/September 2004.

NEGOTIATIONS

Islamic governments have never and will never be established through peaceful solutions and cooperative councils. They are established as they [always] have been by pen and gun, by word and bullet, by tongue and teeth.

Al Qaeda, 10 May 2000.

The confrontation that Islam calls for with these godless and apostate regimes does not know Socratic debates, Platonic ideals, nor Aristotelian diplomacy. But it knows the dialogue of bullets, the ideals of assassination, bombing, and destruction, and the diplomacy of the cannon and machine-gun.

Al Qaeda, 10 May 2000.

The so-called peace agreements with the Jews are false, corrupted, have no value in the Muslim community, since they contradict the book of Allah [Qur'an]...The Jews that kill Muslims will have no remains. Whoever gives them his hand for peace, while they react by shedding the blood of his Muslim brothers, is a coward, ignorant, and has no value towards the brothers of monkeys and pigs.

Sheikh Hamed al-Ali, April 2002.

America knows only the language of force. This is the only way to stop it and make it take its hands off the Muslims and their affairs. America does not know the language of dialogue!! Or the language of peaceful coexistence!! America is kept at bay by blood alone.

Sulaiman Abu Ghaith, 12 June 2002.

The latest manifestation of your fumbling [Saudi government] is that proposal of a one-month opportunity to repent [23 June 2004 government proposal of a month-long period of clemency during which Al Qaeda members could surrender] proposed by your stupid great leader—which means forgiveness for whoever turns himself in…Oh demonic rulers! There is no oath of allegiance between you and us, and we owe you neither hearing nor obeying. There is nothing between us but fighting for the sake of Allah…Oh demonic rulers! We denounce you as infidels, and there is hostility and hatred between us forever until you believe in Allah alone. Oh demonic rulers! There is no surrender, rather fighting; there is no humiliation, rather death; no defeat, rather jihad for the sake of Allah.

Sheik Ubay Abd al-Rahman al-Athari bin Bajad al-'Utaybi, June/July 2004.

Everyone knows that our jihad is for the raising on high of the Creator's Word...and for nothing else...not for a constitution, nor for an accord with the infidel...nor to replace the sword in its scabbard; for our bullets have not run out.

Al Qaeda in Iraq, 21 February 2005.

How can you negotiate with the people who raped our lands and took away our dignity? Have you ever heard of an oppressor who abandoned his oppression because of a conversation? Can any sensible person agree to speak with those who attack them every day and night seeking to kill them?...The only way to respond to oppression is to fight... The infidels can expect nothing from us other than the noises of weapons and the sounds of explosions until they leave our lands and allow us to establish our religious laws.

Al Qaeda in Iraq, 1 May 2005.

NUCLEAR WEAPONS

Acquiring weapons for the defense of Muslims is a religious duty. If I have indeed acquired these weapons, I am carrying out a duty. It would be a sin for Muslims not to try to possess the weapons that would prevent the infidels from inflicting harm on Muslims.

Osama bin Laden, 22 December 1998.

We are pursuing our rights to have them [the Americans] evicted from the Muslim world countries and to prevent them from dominating us. We believe that the right to self-defense is to be enjoyed by all people. Israel is stockpiling hundreds of nuclear warheads and bombs. The Christian West is largely in possession of such weapons. Hence, we do not regard this as a charge, but rather as a right. We do not accept to see anybody level charges against us in this regard. It is as if you were accusing a man of being a courageous knight and fighter. It is as if you were denying him this. Only a man who is not in his right mind would level such accusations. This is a right. We supported the Pakistani people and congratulated them when Allah was gracious enough to enable them to acquire the nuclear weapon. We regard this as one of our rights, of Muslim rights. We disregard such worn-out U.S. charges.

Osama bin Laden, 10 June 1999.

[The movement] will not slacken in its striking of the Americans and the Crusaders in general, right in their very midst, and their burrows, towers and habitations will avail them not...the New York towers still bear witness to that and stand silently from dread of the catastrophe and the magnitude of the deaths...Even their skies and their earth are our target, and they shall learn that we in the Al Qaeda organization are preparing operations ...now that they have refused our Sheikh [Osama]'s truce [offer in April 2004]...and after he warned the American people in his last audio tape not to re-elect the vapid

Bush...we say that this refusal justifies Allah's wrath upon them, so let them wait for what is to come...

Finally, we announce to the Muslim community that production and enrichment associated with nuclear or atomic manufacture is not the monopoly of the Crusaders or Westerners, or the world's tyrants; we are making progress in our efforts to produce bombs, small in volume but big in impact.

Abu Anas al-Maghribi, 9 November 2004.

OIL

As for oil, it is a commodity that will be subject to the price of the market according to supply and demand. We believe that the current prices are not realistic due to the Saudi regime playing the role of a U.S. agent and the pressures exercised by the U.S. on the Saudi regime to increase production and flooding the market that caused a sharp decrease in oil prices.

Osama bin Laden, March 1997.

He (Bush) is concealing his own ambitions and the ambitions of the Zionist lobby and their own desire for oil. He is still following the mentality of his ancestors who killed the Native Americans to take their land and wealth. He thought that this time [invasion of Iraq] it would be an easy task and a lie that would not be exposed.

Osama bin Laden, 18 October 2003.

The Jewish-Christian coalition, led by the U.S., must not even dream of taking over the Muslims' oil in Iraq and in the Arabian Peninsula. Otherwise—if Allah so wills it—sacrifices will be made, bodies will be torn limb from limb and blood will flow.

Salim al-Makhi, "Mending the Hearts of the Believers." October/November 2002.

The occupation of Iraq is a link in the Zionist-Crusader chain of evil. Then comes the full occuparion of the rest of the Gulf States to set the stage for controlling and dominating the whole world. For the big powers believe that the Gulf and the Gulf States are the keys to global control due to the presence of the largest oil reserves there. The situation is serious and the misfortune momentous...Today they have robbed you of Baghdad, and tomorrow they will rob you of Riyadh, unless Allah deems otherwise.

Osama bin Laden, 4 January 2004.

The Sheikh [Osama bin Laden] expects that the U.S. will directly attack the oil sources and will declare their occupation. This situation will lead to a total collapse of the regimes of the region...America will prefer direct occupation only in two scenarios:
1) The collapse of these regimes, and primarily the [Saudi]

regime...Then America will enter in order to secure what it thinks are its direct interests.

2) America will take a mighty blow, will go berserk, and will decide to punish the extremists deep in the Arabian Peninsula, by means of direct occupation

Louis Attiya Allah, 20 January 2004.

One of the main causes of our enemies' gaining hegemony over our country is their stealing our oil; therefore, you [Mujahideen in Iraq] should make every effort in your power to stop the greatest theft in history of the natural resources of both present and future generations, which is being carried out through collaboration between foreigners and [native] agents... Focus your operations on it [oil production], especially in Iraq and the Gulf area, since this [lack of oil] will cause them to die off [on their own].

Osama bin Laden, 27 December 2004.

PAKISTAN

There is no doubt that we have been pleased and heartened by the wide-spread Islamic response across the whole Muslim world, and in particular, on the part of the people of Pakistan. They have been very effective in their movement...there are some governmental departments, which, by the grace of Allah, respond to the Islamic sentiments of the masses in Pakistan. This is reflected in sympathy and cooperation. However, some other governmental departments fell into the trap of the infidels who committed aggression against the Ancient House and the Holy Ka'ba.

Osama bin Laden, 22 December 1998.

The U.S. has a dream to take the Indian subcontinent shared by her friends, namely India and Israel. It seeks to destroy the Islamic thoughts, feelings and emotions in the hearts and minds of the Muslims as well as to destroy the nuclear capability of the Muslims in Pakistan.

Fatwa on General Pervez Musharraf and the U.S.A., 16 September 2001.

It's not a surprise that the Muslim community in Pakistan will die defending Islam. It is considered on the front line of defending Islam, as Afghanistan was on the front line of defending itself and Pakistan during the Russian invasion more than 20 years ago. We hope that these brothers will be the first martyrs in the battle of Islam in this era against the new Jewish and Christian Crusader campaign that is led by the Chief Crusader Bush under the banner of the cross. We tell our Muslim brothers in Pakistan to use all their means to resist the invasion of the American Crusader forces in Pakistan and Afghanistan.

Osama bin Laden, 24 September 2001.

Pakistan is a great hope for the Islamic brotherhood. Its people are awakened, organized and rich in the spirit of faith. They backed Afghanistan in its war against the Soviet Union and extended every help to the Mujahideen and the Afghan people. Then these are the very Pakistanis who are standing shoulder to shoulder with the Taliban. If such people emerge in just two countries, the domination of the West will diminish in a matter of days...Pakistan is sacred for us like a place of worship. We are the people of jihad and fighting for the defense of Pakistan is the best of all jihads to us.

Osama bin Laden, 28 September 2001.

The government of Pakistan should have the wishes of the people in view. It should not have surrendered to the unjustified demands of America. America does not have solid proof against us. It just has some surmises. It is unjust to start bombing on the basis of those surmises...We will not leave the Pakistani people and the Pakistani territory at anybody's mercy. We will defend Pakistan. But we have been disappointed by Gen. Pervez Musharraf. He says that the majority is with him. I say the majority is against him.

Osama bin Laden, 7 November 2001.

It is [President Pervez] Musharraf who enabled America to topple the [Taliban's] Islamic emirate in Afghanistan. Had it not been for his tremendous help, America would not have been able to do this, nor would it have been able to kill thousands of innocents in Afghanistan. It is Musharraf who is seeking to send Pakistani forces to Iraq so that they, rather than American soldiers, are killed and so that they kill Muslims in Iraq and enable America to control Muslim lands. Muslims in Pakistan must unite and co-operate to topple this traitor and install a sincere leadership that would defend Islam and Muslims.

Ayman al-Zawahiri, 28 September 2003.

PALESTINE/PALESTINIANS

[The Americans] accuse our children in Palestine of being terrorists, those children that have no weapons and have not even reached maturity. At the same time they defend a country with its airplanes and tanks, and the state of the Jews that has a policy to destroy the future of these children.

Osama bin Laden, 28 May 1998.

Sometimes we find the right elements to push for one cause more than the other. Last year's blessed intifada helped us to push more for the Palestinian issue. This push helps the other cause. Attacking America helps the cause of Palestine and vice versa. There is no conflict between the two; on the contrary, one serves the other.

Osama bin Laden, 21 October 2001.

How can the weak mothers in Palestine endure the killing of their children in front of their eyes by the unjust Jewish executioners with U.S. support and with U.S. aircraft and tanks? Those who distinguish between America and Israel are the real enemies of the Muslim community. They are traitors who betrayed Allah and His Prophet [Muhammad], and who betrayed their Muslim community and the trust placed in them. They anesthetize the Muslim community.

Osama bin Laden, 3 November 2001.

[Bin Laden] serves the Palestinian issue by attacking the American interests, since Israel is one of America's allies in the Muslim world, and there is no distinction between America and Zionism.

Abu Ayman al-Hilali, December 2001.

Studies of the Mujahideen in Palestine show that they need more support. For example, rear bases for the Mujahideen need to be established in all countries. An attempt must be made to penetrate the borders with Palestine and bring in weapons. Military operations must be carried out against the Zionists, their sponsors and their domesticated clients.

Abu Ubayd al-Qurashi, 8 October 2002.

The blood pouring out of Palestine must be equally revenged. You must know that the Palestinians do not cry alone; their women are not widowed alone; their sons are not orphaned alone.

Al Qaeda, 24 November 2002.

Brothers in Islam: From the land of the Night Journey and the Ascension to Heaven [Palestine], we announce to the Islamic community the establishment of the Islamic Al Qaeda Organization in Palestine, which will serve as a powerful basis for restoring the rights of our Arab and Islamic people in Palestine, [and] will defeat the Zionist Jewish invaders [and] return them to the place from whence they came...Islamic Al Qaeda in Palestine joins its voice with the voices of the Mujahideen in Palestine in its resistance to the partial and submissive solutions, and will accept nothing but the full liberation of the Palestinian land...we call to the Mujahideen... to immediately stop the fighting between Hamas and the people of the Palestinian Authority, because these deeds serve only the murderous Jews, the Great Satans...Death to the Jews and Zionism.

Abu Banan, 4 December 2002.

In Palestine we are not only facing the Jews but also the anti-Islam international alliance headed by the U.S. Crusaders. So, fighting the Jews and leaving America without being attacked will not make the Americans or the Crusaders lessen their aggression against us.

Ayman al-Zawahiri, 1 October 2004.

PALESTINIAN LIBERATION
ORGANIZATION (PLO)

Those who sympathize with the infidels, such as the PLO in Palestine, or the so-called Palestinian Authority, have been trying for tens of years to get back some of their rights, and they laid down their arms and abandoned what is called 'violence' these days, and ran after peaceful bargaining. But what did the Jews give them? They did not give them even 1% of their rights. Even the Gaza Airport and the so-called Palestinian Authority are under the mercy of their guns and under the control of the Jewish security forces.

Osama bin Laden, 22 December 1998.

PHILIPPINES

It [the United States] was also the chief supporter of the Crusader regime in the Philippines in order to remove our Muslim brothers present there.

Al Qaeda, 24 April 2002.

We call on all believers in the oneness of Allah, who fear the day of judgment, to do their sacred duty to protect the interests of Islam and strike at its enemies, both foreign and local, at their persons and their properties wherever they may be.

Khadaffy Janjalani, 27 September 2002.

POLICE INTERROGATION

If unfortunately, a friend is arrested, he should remember two things: do not assume that the police know everything because they do not and always try to protect your friends and colleagues...The police may try to make you believe that they already know everything, and that if you lie or try to hide information from them, you will unnecessarily expose yourself to torture...The place you are arrested from is important. If you are arrested at home, you will face a different set of questions than those arrested from a place of operation or from a Mujahideen hideout...While being interrogated, try to guess if the interrogator suspects that you are a Mujahid or if he knows you are one. Vary your responses accordingly...the investigators are humans like you, so do not let them bully you or enjoy unnecessary influence over you...The key point is: you are not guilty unless proven, so do not let your answers [be used] as evidence against you. Do not let your answers lead the interrogators to other friends.

Al Qaeda, January 2004.

POLITICAL PROGRAM

Al Qaeda has no political program compatible with the existing world order, simply because the existing world order does not recognize us as an independent Islamic state, and forces us to be its satellite, to adapt ourselves to its secular laws, and to be subjugated to its military rule. Al Qaeda is absolutely opposed to this, and states: The world order must be removed from the region and defeated, first of all militarily. Then, the Islamic state must be reestablished, in accordance with the Islamic regime. This means that we will control our fate, rule over ourselves, and control our resources...

No political program has a chance of succeeding if we do not defeat the West, militarily and culturally, and remove it from Muslim countries...We will become the masters of the world, as the world's economic fate depends on us because we have the resources the world needs and all the elements of controlling the world are in our hands. What we are lacking is to live free and to rule ourselves by ourselves, cut off from the West and its agents.

Louis Attiya Allah, December 2003.

The Islamic State will not arise through means of slogans, demonstrations, parties, and elections, but through blood, body parts, and [the sacrifice] of lives.

Nabil Sahraoui, 9 January 2004.

POLLUTION

You [the United States] have destroyed nature with your industrial waste and gases more than any other nation in history.

Al Qaeda, 24 November 2002.

PRISONERS

We have said in the past, and continue to say, that we are treating the [American] prisoners according to Shari'a that demands we show mercy to prisoners regardless of their nationality or their actions during this conflict. We will not treat these prisoners as the Americans have treated our prisoners at Guantanamo Bay which Al Jazeera TV has clearly broadcast. We don't beat prisoners, and I am sure, if the American people saw the prisoners here with us, they would be confused and probably wouldn't think they were prisoners at all.

Taliban Military Commander, 2 April 2002.

REFORM

True reform is based on three principles:

The first principle is the rule of Shari'a, because Shari'a, which was given by Allah, protects the believers' interests, freedom, honor, and pride, and protects what is sacred to them. The Islamic nation will not accept any other law, after it has suffered from the anti-Islamic trends forcefully imposed on it.

The second principle of reform is the freedom of the lands of Islam. No reform is conceivable while our countries are occupied by the Crusader forces, which are spread throughout our countries. No reform is conceivable while the Crusader forces are stationed in our countries [where they] enjoy support, supplies, and storage facilities, and go forth from our countries to attack our brothers and sisters in other Islamic countries. No reform is conceivable while our governments are controlled by the American embassies, which stick their noses into all our affairs.

The third principle of reform is the Muslim nation's freedom to run its own affairs. This [principle of] reform will only be realized in two ways. First, freedom of the independent religious judicial system, the implementation of its rulings, and the guaranteeing of its honor, authority and strength. Second, the freedom and the right of the Islamic nation to implement the principle of 'promoting virtue and preventing vice.'

Ayman al-Zawahiri, 17 June 2005.

RELIGIOUS TOLERANCE

Muslims should consider with care the verses on loyalty, faith and jihad. They should sever any relations with the Jews and the Christians...whoever befriends Jews and Christians becomes like them, and becomes one of them in their religion and in their infidelity.

Osama bin Laden, 22 December 1998.

Islam does not coincide or make a truce with unbelief, but rather confronts it.

Al Qaeda, 10 May 2000.

It is the United States which is perpetrating every maltreatment on women, children and common people of other faiths, particularly the followers of Islam...Only one conclusion could be derived from the indifference of the United States and the West to these acts of terror and the patronage of the tyrants by these powers—America is an anti-Islamic power, and it is patronizing the anti-Islamic forces. Its friendship with the Muslim countries is just a show and deceitful.

Osama bin Laden, 28 September 2001.

It is impermissible to co-operate with Jews and Christians, and he who co-operates with them, gives them his opinion, or takes actions in supporting them becomes an apostate and revokes his faith in Allah and His Prophet [Muhammad].
Sulaiman Abu Ghaith, 13 October 2001.

The war that America has led against our lands is only a part of the war against Islam. Verily America, when it declared war against Afghanistan, wanted primarily to remove the Islamic system and the ruling of the Shari'a and the prevention of the revival of the Islamic religion that it is afraid of.

Mullah Omar, 16 September 2002.

Even in America, the head of unbelief and the greatest enemy of Islam and the Muslims, the centers of preaching are still open. But just because they exist does not mean that it is permitted to halt the jihad against America while it kills the Muslims and occupies their lands, defends Israel, and preserves it [Israel] from its enemies.

Editorial Board, *The Voice of Jihad*, 20 January 2004.

At the beginning of any jihad military operation, it is not advisable to target religious places unless they are used for:

1. Missionaries in Islamic countries, where they try to convert Muslims to Christians, such as what happened in Yemen and as what is going on in Iraq as well as what was going on in the Land of the Two Holy Mosques, where they were distributing Bibles to homes. In this case hunting those people is good, and we know who they are.

2. Covert intelligence operations. Any Muslim religious scholar who cooperates with the enemy. Targeting those is glorified and makes them as symbols for Allah's anger.

3. Reverends, priests, rabbis and any religious personality that attack Islam or Muslims, such as an American reverend that cursed the Prophet, we hope to Allah that we will get his neck...

4. Any (Jewish or Christian) personality that provides financial, military, or moral support against Muslims, as with what happened with the Crusades in the past.

Abdul Aziz al-Muqrin, 29 March 2004.

RELIGIOUS WAR

The U.S. is at war with Muslims. They have committed various atrocities against the Muslim community, ranging from killing, raping our honor and land, mass murders in Iraq, funding and assisting the establishment of Israel, violating the sanctity of Muslims in Iraq, and controlling Muslim land, sea and air space. The U.S. is not only targeting the military but also civil areas in the Muslim land of Iraq.

Fatwa on General Pervez Musharraf and the U.S.A., 16 September 2001.

This war is fundamentally religious. The people of the East are Muslims. They sympathize with Muslims against the people of the West, who are the Crusaders. Those who try to cover this crystal clear fact, which the entire world has admitted, are deceiving the Muslim community. They are trying to deflect the attention of the Muslim community from the truth of this conflict...Under no circumstances should we forget this enmity between us and the infidels. For, the enmity is based on creed. We must be loyal to the believers and those who believe that there is no God but Allah. We should also renounce the atheists and infidels. It suffices me to seek Allah's help against them.

Osama bin Laden, 3 November 2001.

How can we forget that the very name Israel—which is supported by the United States—is based on a religious belief…It [Israel] captures our land and kills our children and women on a religious basis, as they claim. It considers Jerusalem its eternal capital on a religious basis. It calls on the United States to transfer its capital [embassy] to Jerusalem on a religious basis. After all this, the United States claims that its campaign against jihad—which it terms terrorism—and in defense of Israel is not a religious war.

Ayman al-Zawahiri, 9 November 2001.

The war between us and unbelief and the people of unbelief is a war between two unequal forces. They surpass us in material preparedness, and we surpass them with the preparedness of belief and courageous resolve.

Abu Abd al-Rahman al-Turkemani, December 2003.

The conflict in the world today is a conflict between belief and unbelief. The war in Palestine, in Afghanistan, in Iraq, in Algeria, in Chechnya, and in the Philippines is one war. This is a war between the camp of Islam and the camp of the Cross, to which the Americans, Zionists, Jews, their apostate allies and others belong.

Nabil Sahraoui, 9 January 2004.

It is a conflict between world heresy—and with it today's apostates—under the leadership of America on the one hand,

and on the other, the Muslim community with the brigades of Mujahideen in its vanguard.

Osama bin Laden, 27 December 2004.

RUSSIA

We went through vicious battles with the Russians. It is enough to just say with Russians, they are known in the West for their brutality and viciousness.

Osama bin Laden, 28 May 1998.

In the past when Al Qaeda fought with the Mujahideen, we were asked, "Can you defeat the Soviet Union?" The Soviet Union scared the whole world then. NATO used to tremble in fear of the Soviet Union. Where is that power now? We barely remember it. It broke down into many small states, and Russia remained.

Osama bin Laden, 21 October 2001.

What crime have the Muslims of Chechnya, Afghanistan, and the Republics of Central Asia committed that the tyrannical Crusader Soviet military machine, followed by the Communist one, can sweep them away and then kill, destroy, and remove tens of thousands of them?

Al Qaeda, 24 April 2002.

If you were distressed by the killing of your nationals in Moscow [Moscow theater siege, October 2002], remember ours in Chechnya.

Osama bin Laden, 12 November 2002.

The Mujahideen are trying to escalate the operations in order to topple [President] Putin, Allah willing. Putin is trying by any and all means to present himself during these months as a victor in order to win the elections.

Sheikh Abu Omar al-Sayf, 31 December 2003.

Our Mujahideen managed to hijack two Russian planes... and have succeeded in directing the first attack [female suicide bombings of two Russian passenger jets on 24 August], which will be followed by a series of other operations in the hopes of providing a wave of support and aid to our Muslim brothers in Chechnya and other enslaved regions that suffer from Russian disbelief.

Al-Islambouli Brigades, 26 August 2004.

We are notifying everyone that by the mercy of Allah the Military Council of Kabardino-Balkaria Yarmuk has been formed today. Units of Yarmuk have been deployed all across the territory of Kabardino-Balkaria [a constituent republic of the Russian Federation north of Georgia and west of Chechnya] and are now starting to carry out the assigned combat missions in accordance with the requirements of jihad...On their orders our mosques are getting closed down...a ban is put on spreading of the religion of Islam ...ordinary Muslims of Karbardino-Balkaria are not allowed in the mosque without having special permission.

Information Council of Karbardino-Balkarian Islamic Jammat 'Yarmuk', 31 August 2004.

Who is responsible for the attacks on Rusnya [derogatory word for Russia]? By the Grace of Allah, the martyr battalion, Riyad us-Saliheen [Gardens of the Righteous] has carried out several successful operations on the territory of Rusnya.

The regional martyr unit of Moscow was responsible for the blasts on Kashirskoye Road [near Domodedovo Airport] and the Rizhskaya metro station in Moscow. The downing of the [Tu-134 and Tu-154] airliners [which left from Domodedovo] was carried out by the special operations unit.

And the second battalion, under the command of Col. Orstkhoyev, was responsible for the "Nord-Vest" operation in Beslan [pun on the Moscow Dubrovka theater siege, where the musical Nord-Ost was playing].

Putin screamed like a scolded pig...What happened in Beslan is a terrible tragedy: the bloodsucker from the Kremlin killed or wounded 1,000 children and adults by ordering the storming of the school to satisfy his imperial ambitions and to keep his job. In the most impudent manner Putin is now trying to blame us for that, accusing us also of international terrorism and appealing to the world for help.

We demand that the war in Chechnya be stopped immediately and that the withdrawal of forces be carried out. We insist that Putin immediately resign from his post as president of the Russian Federation...

I have not met bin Laden. I received no money from him, but I would not have declined the offer.

Shamil Basayev, 17 September 2004.

SADDAM HUSSEIN

We, as Muslims, do not like the Iraqi regime, but we think that the Iraqi people and their children are our brothers, and we care about their future.

Osama bin Laden, 10 July 1996.

They [Arab regimes] feared that the door would be open for bringing down dictatorial regimes by armed forces from abroad, especially after they had seen the arrest of their former comrade [Saddam Hussein] in treason and agentry to the United States, when it [U.S.] ordered him to ignite the first Gulf war against Iran, which had rebelled against it [U.S.].

Osama bin Laden, 4 January 2004.

The comparison between Osama bin Laden and Saddam Hussein is not an apt one, since Saddam has some dark chapters in his past conduct toward his people—just look at the massacre of the Kurds in Halabja, the massacre of the Shi'ites in the south, the violation of Iraqi women, the anarchy, the despotism, and the enslavement of the Iraqi people; [all these factors] caused him to be hated and that made his arrest easier. But Osama bin Laden, wherever you go from one corner of the world to another...he is popular and well-received.

Nasser Ahmad Nasser al-Bahri, 3 August 2004.

In Iraq itself, the apostate tyrant Saddam Hussein stood at the head of the government of the Baath Party.

Abd al-Rahman ibn Salem al-Shamari, August/September 2004.

Indeed, Saddam is a thief and an apostate, but the solution should never have been to transfer Iraq from the indigenous thief to the foreign thief. Helping the infidel to rob the Muslims' land and to gain control over them is an act that removes one from Islam.

Osama bin Laden, 27 December 2004.

SAUDI ARABIA

The main reason for writing this letter to you [King Fahd of Saudi Arabia] is not your oppression of people and their rights (especially the scholars, the callers to righteousness, the merchants, and the senior chiefs of tribes). It's not your insult to the dignity of our nation, your desecration of its sanctuaries, and your embezzlement of its wealth and riches. It's not what has been spread during your reign of bribery, forging, and disintegration of management and morals. It's not the economic breakdown that has hit the country and almost made it reach the level of bankruptcy...The quintessence of our dispute is the fact that your ruling system has transgressed 'There is no God but Allah.'

Osama bin Laden, 3 August 1995.

Ignoring the divine Shari'a law, depriving people of their legitimate rights, allowing the Americans to occupy the Land of the Two Holy Mosques; imprisonment, unjustly, of the sincere scholars...Through its course of actions the regime has torn off its legitimacy... The situation in the Land of the Two Holy Mosques has become like a huge volcano on the verge of eruption that would destroy the infidels and the corruption and its sources. The explosion at Riyadh [13 November 1995] and al-Khobar [25 June 1996] is a warning of this volcanic eruption emerging as a result of the severe oppression, suffering, excessive iniquity, humiliation and poverty.

Osama bin Laden, 23 August 1996.

The majority of the nation, both civilians and military individuals, are aware of the wicked plan. They refused to be played against each other and to be used by the regime as a tool to carry out the policy of the American-Israeli alliance through their agent in our country: the Saudi regime.

Osama bin Laden, 23 August 1996.

The [Saudi] regime does not cease to cry in the open over the matters affecting the Muslims, without making any serious effort to serve the interests of the Muslim community, apart from small efforts, in order to confuse people and throw some dust into their eyes.

Osama bin Laden, October/November 1996.

This big mistake by the Saudi regime of inviting the American troops revealed their deception. They have given their support to nations that have been fighting against Muslims. They helped the Yemeni Communists against the southern Yemeni Muslims and are helping [Yasser] Arafat's regime fight Hamas. After it insulted and jailed the Islamic clerics 18 months ago, the Saudi regime lost its legitimacy... our country has become an American colony.

Osama bin Laden, 6 December 1996.

Regarding the criticisms of the ruling regime in Saudi Arabia and the Arabian Peninsula, the first one is their subordination to the U.S. So, our main problem is the U.S. government, while the Saudi regime is but a branch or an agent of the U.S. By being loyal to the U.S. regime, the Saudi regime has committed an act against Islam. And this, based on the ruling of Shari'a, casts the regime outside the religious community.

Osama bin Laden, March 1997.

For over seven years the United States has been occupying the lands of Islam in the holiest of places, the Arabian Peninsula, plundering its riches, dictating to its rulers, humiliating its people, terrorizing its neighbors, and turning its bases in the peninsula into a spearhead through which to fight the neighboring Muslim peoples.

World Islamic Front for Jihad against the Jews and Crusaders, 23 February 1998.

You [America] will leave [Saudi Arabia] when the youth send you the wooden boxes and the coffins, and you will carry in them the bodies of American troops and civilians. This is when you will leave.

Osama bin Laden, 28 May 1998.

[The attack on Western housing complexes in Riyadh on 12 May 2003] was but the opening shot, Allah willing, and the

Mujahideen had a need for this detailed communiqué to present the reasons for the jihad activity in the Arabian Peninsula and to remove some of the religious and military problems regarding it...This operation reminded the Americans that they cannot dream of security before the Muslims in Palestine experience it, and before all Crusader countries leave the peninsula of the Prophet Muhammad.

Al Qaeda in Saudi Arabia, 3 September 2003.

It is true that we must keep the enemy preoccupied with himself and not give him a sense of security, because as soon as he secures his bases and his lines of supply, he will have an opportunity to use them to attack our brothers in different parts of the countries of the Islamic world...It is also true that we must take advantage of this country [Saudi Arabia] because it is the primary source of funds for most jihad movements, and it has some degree of security and freedom of movement. But we must strike a balance between this and America's invasion of the Islamic world and its hobbling of the jihad movement and even of other Islamic movements.

Abu Hajjer, October 2003.

One of the greatest places in which jihad is a commandment applying to each Muslim individually is the Land of the Two Holy Mosques. In this land there is the occupying Crusader enemy who steals the land's treasures, determines its policy, and sets out from it to make war on the Muslims. It also has an apostate agent government, and it implements the plans of colonialism, supports the infidels, and rules by a law that is not the law of Allah.

Sulaiman al-Dosari, *The Voice of Jihad*, no . 1, October 2003.

Our war with the enemies of Allah continues everywhere... We will not let the Americans occupy the Land of the Two Holy Mosques [and feel] secure and safe, and we will not cease our jihad until we liberate every inch of Muslim land...We must guard ourselves against...confrontations with the armies and forces of the state, so that we can strike lethal blows to the occupiers, Allah willing.

This does not mean we will surrender to those who defend the Crusaders if they attack us; on the contrary, in this case we must resist with all the strength we have, and we must punish them so that they turn their swords toward the Americans and fight among our ranks, or refrain from entering [into] a confrontation with us—or they will stand against us and wait for what lies in store for them [at our hands], thanks to Allah and with His strength.

Sulaiman al-Dosari, *The Voice of Jihad*, no. 2, October 2003.

The regime of the al-Sa'ud tribe [Saudi Arabia]...continues to mislead the people and claim that it loves the wisdom and clerics of the religion, and loves to serve the religion...This is a false claim and an act of deceit directed at the servants of Allah.

Muhammad bin Shazzaf al-Shahri, 17 October 2003.

Igniting the fire in the Arabian Peninsula is expected to be one of the keys to the great change, because the Arabian Peninsula is the heart, and any change in the Arabian Peninsula affects the other parts of the Islamic body.

Louis Attiya Allah, December 2003.

Since our brothers in Al Qaeda are preoccupied with waging war on the Crusaders, and since it has become clear from their repeated communiqués that they are not attacking the internal security apparatus, we have decided to relieve them of this important [religious obligation] and to purge the Land of the Two Holy Mosques of the [Arab] agents, freeing [Al Qaeda] to purge it of the Crusaders.

Al-Haramain Brigades, 5 December 2003.

I recommend to the Mujahideen that instead of engaging in clashes and warfare against the Saudi government, it is better to go to Iraq. There, there are weapons aplenty, and there they can fight the Americans. It is no secret that great damage will be caused the Americans if the Mujahideen turn to Iraq to fight them.

Sheikh Abu Omar al-Sayf, 31 December 2003.

Today the House of Saud is doing everything it can to fulfill the Crusaders' demands and disarm the people of the Arabian Peninsula...This is another chapter in the deceitful series by the triple axis of corruption—the Jews, the Crusaders and the House of Saud—whose aim is to bring the people of the Arabian Peninsula into a vicious cycle of weakness in a way that will affect their struggle with the occupying invaders, so that when they want to defend their religion and their honor, they will find nothing but stones and curses...The throne of the House of Saud is on the rim of the volcano under which the pot is boiling.

Sheikh Abdallah al-Rashoud, 20 January 2004.

In our jihad in the Arabian Peninsula, we are serving the Iraqi cause and helping the Mujahideen there with whom we are in constant contact and are supporting.

Abdul Aziz al-Muqrin, 14 May 2004.

Every special thing to these Crusaders from their communities, their bases, and means of transport, especially the Western and American aviation companies, will be a direct target for our coming operations...we are reaffirming and repeating this notice and our calls and our advice to our Muslim brothers...And we urge them not to mingle with the American and Western Crusaders and the rest of the infidels in the Arabian Peninsula. And also we renew the warning to individuals of the security forces and guards of the Crusader compounds and the American bases and all those who stand in ranks with America, its agents, opponents of the Mujahideen... we call on them to repent and separate themselves from the heretics.

Al Qaeda in the Arabian Peninsula, 6 June 2004.

But one must ask the question: what causes these youth to take up arms and to commit bombings on Saudi soil? I think that it is the stupid policies of the Saudi government regarding these people...The operations in Saudi Arabia were reactions [against the Saudi government].

Nasser Ahmad Nasser al-Bahri, 3 August 2004.

It has been claimed that the Mujahideen are responsible for that which has befallen Saudi Arabia. However, the self-evident truth is that the responsibility falls on the shoulders of the regime, which has neglected the conditions necessary for guaranteeing security, life, harmonious relations, and social cohesion...[The regime] has allied itself with infidel America and helped it [in its war] against Muslims If...the ruler becomes an apostate and abandons Allah's law, it is incumbent upon the subjects, by Allah's command, to rebel. Obedience to him is not absolute, but rather is conditional upon his probity.
Osama bin Laden, 27 December 2004.

The government of Riyadh joined a world alliance with the Crusader heresy under the leadership of [President George] Bush against Islam and its people...They opened their bases to American forces in order to invade Iraq...And now, they have shown us a new chapter in the series of conspiracies with America, which they call 'the initiative of sending Arab and Muslim forces for peacekeeping in Iraq'...With this initiative, they seek to legitimize the American occupation.

Osama bin Laden, 27 December 2004.

SECULARISM

There is no doubt that one of the greatest threats to the hegemony of Islam and the dominance of Shari'a is the American secularism that will be imposed forcefully on the region...The Islamic world will change from dictatorship to democracy, which means subhuman degradation in all walks of life.

Al Qaeda, 25 April 2003.

The conflict is a conflict between two ways, and a deep struggle between two beliefs: a conflict between the divine, perfect way, submitting full authority to Allah in all matters... and the grossly secular way.

Osama bin Laden, 27 December 2004.

SEPTEMBER 11, 2001

Americans will not be able to prevent such acts like the one that has just occurred because America has taken Islam hostage. If you look at Islamic countries, the people are in despair. They are complaining that Islam is gone. But people remain firm in their Islamic beliefs. In their pain and frustration, some of them commit suicide acts. They feel they have nothing to lose.

Mullah Omar, 21 September 2001.

I have already said that I am not involved in the 11 September attacks in the United States. As a Muslim, I try my best to avoid telling a lie. I had no knowledge of these attacks, nor do I consider the killing of innocent women, children and other humans as an appreciable act. Islam strictly forbids causing harm to innocent women, children and other people. Such a practice is forbidden even in the course of a battle.

Osama bin Laden, 28 September 2001.

The United States should try to trace the perpetrators of these attacks within itself; the people who are a part of the U.S. system, but are dissenting against it, or those who are working for some other system; persons who want to make the present century as a century of conflict between Islam and Christianity so that their own civilization, nation, country, or ideology could survive. They can be anyone, from Russia to Israel and from India to Serbia. In the U.S. itself, there are dozens of well-organized and well-equipped groups which are capable of causing a large-scale destruction. Then you cannot forget the American Jews, who have been annoyed with President Bush ever since the elections in Florida and want to get revenge...Is it not that there exists a government within the government in the United States? That secret government must be asked who carried out the attacks.

Osama bin Laden, 28 September 2001.

Cleanse your heart and purify it and forget everything involving this secular life, for the time for playing is gone and it is now the time for truth...Let your chest be open because it's only moments before you begin a happy life and eternal bliss with the Prophets and the veracious and martyrs and the righteous, and these are the best of companions...Don't manifest any hesitation and control yourself and be joyful with ease, because you are embarking upon a mission that Allah is pleased with. And you will be rewarded by living with the inhabitants of heaven...And then when the zero-hour comes, open your chest and welcome death in the cause of Allah, always remembering your prayers to ease your mission before the goal in seconds. And let your last words be, 'There is no God but Allah and Muhammad is His Messenger.' And then comes the meeting in the Highest Paradise with the mercy of Allah.

9/11 Hijackers, 29 September 2001.

There is America, hit by Allah in one of its softest spots. Its greatest buildings were destroyed, thank Allah for that. There is America, full of fear from its north to its south, from its west to its east. Thank Allah for that. What America is tasting now is something insignificant compared to what we have tasted for scores of years. Our Muslim community has been tasting this humiliation and this degradation for more than 80 years. Its sons are killed, its blood is shed, its sanctuaries are attacked, and no one hears and no one heeds. When Allah blessed one of the groups of Islam, vanguards of Islam, they destroyed America. I pray to Allah to elevate their status and bless them.

Osama bin Laden, 7 October 2001.

The actions by these young men who destroyed the United States and launched the storm of planes against it have done a good deed. They transferred the battle into the U.S. heartland. Let the United States know that with Allah's permission, the battle will continue to be waged on its territory until it leaves our lands, stops it support for the Jews, and lifts the unjust embargo on the Iraqi people who have lost more than one million children. The Americans should know that the storm of plane attacks will not abate, with Allah's permission. There are thousands of the Muslim community's youths who are eager to die just as the Americans are eager to live.

Sulaiman Abu Ghaith, 9 October 2001.

The events of Tuesday, September the 11th, in New York and Washington are great on all levels. Their repercussions are not over. Although the collapse of the Twin Towers is huge,

THE WORLD ACCORDING TO AL QAEDA

but the events that followed, and I'm not just talking about the economic repercussions, those are continuing, the events that followed are dangerous and more enormous than the collapse of the Towers. The values of this Western civilization under the leadership of America have been destroyed. Those awesome symbolic Towers that speak of liberty, human rights, and humanity have been destroyed. They have gone up in smoke.

Osama bin Laden, 21 October 2001.

The Towers were an economic power and not a children's school. Those that were there were men who supported the biggest economic power in the world. They have to review their books. We will do as they do. If they kill our women and our innocent people, we will kill their women and their innocent people until they stop.

Osama bin Laden, 21 October 2001.

Those men who sacrificed themselves in New York and Washington, they are the spokesmen of the Muslim community's conscience. They are the Muslim community's conscience that saw they had to avenge against the oppression.

Osama bin Laden, 21 October 2001.

America and its allies are massacring us in Palestine, Chechnya, Kashmir and Iraq. The Muslims have the right to attack America in reprisal...The September 11 attacks were

186

not targeted at women and children. The real targets were America's icons of military and economic power.

Osama bin Laden, 7 November 2001.

We calculated in advance the number of casualties from the enemy, who would be killed based on the position of the tower. We calculated that the floors that would be hit would be three or four floors. I was the most optimistic of all...Due to my experience in this field, I was thinking that the fire from the fuel in the plane would melt the iron structure of the building and collapse the area where the plane hit and the floors above it only. This is all we had hoped for...The brothers, who conducted the operation, all they knew was that they had a martyrdom operation, and we asked each of them to go to America. They didn't know anything about the operation, not even one letter. But they were trained, and we did not reveal the operation to them until they were there [in the U.S.] and just before they boarded the planes...Those who were trained to fly didn't know the others. One group of people did not know the other group.

Osama bin Laden, ca. 9 November 2001.

Those people found a security breach as big as a whole fleet of hijacked civilian aircraft, and managed to shove America's nose into the ground, to strike it with this lightning, to take it by surprise, and to strike it with the greatest military, security, political and economic blows...I cannot conceal the fact that we here in Afghanistan, like hundreds of millions of Muslims throughout the world, could not contain our joy when we saw America taste, for one day, what the Islamic people have been swallowing every day for decades because of the actions of the U.S., both directly and indirectly. We rejoiced at this. Although we did not carry them out, these blows coincided with our interests, and their results were significant for us.

Mahfouz Walad al-Walid, 30 November 2001.

These blessed and successful strikes are reactions to what is happening on our land in Palestine, Iraq and elsewhere... They shook America's throne and struck at the U.S. economy in the heart. They struck the largest military power deep in the heart...this international usurious, damnable economy—which America uses along with its military power to impose infidelity and humiliation on weak people—can easily collapse...they taught those arrogant people, who see freedom as meaningless if not belonging to the white race, a tough lesson. These people believe that other people must be humiliated and enslaved.

Osama bin Laden, 26 December 2001.

Al Qaeda takes pride in that, on September 11, it destroyed the elements of America's strategic defense, which the former U.S.S.R. and every other hostile state could not harm...With the September 11 attack, Al Qaeda entered the annals of successful surprise attacks...Moreover, in the pain it caused, [Al Qaeda] surpassed these surprise attacks, because it put every individual in American society on [constant] alert for every possibility, whether emotionally or practically.

Abu Ubayd al-Qurashi, January/February 2002.

We wanted to send the message written in the color of blood...the essence of the message is that the time of bondage and humiliation is over, and the time has come to kill the Americans at home and penetrate their forces and their intelligence...We killed them [Americans] away from their home, and today we kill them on their soil. May Allah accept me as a martyr.

Ahmed al-Haznawi, 9/11 hijacker, 15 April 2002.

Those 19 hijackers who went out and worked and sacrificed their lives for Allah, Allah granted their conquest that we enjoy today. The great victory that was achieved was because of Allah's help and not because of our efficiency or power.

Ayman al-Zawahiri, 15 April 2002.

Allah has given success to a group of young men of Islam with his favor and generosity, and has shown his prosperity and kindness because he has restored to the Muslim community some of its truth. He has made the Crusader enemy drink from the cup that they made us drink from for decades and decades. The heroes who offered themselves for the destruction of the strongholds of the enemy did not offer themselves in order to gain earthly possessions, or temporary fame, or a transitory desire. Rather, they offered their souls as a sacrifice for the religion of Allah Almighty, defending Muslims whom American hands had mistreated by various types of torture and forms of domination and subjugation in every place...the only motive these young men had was to defend the religion of Allah, their dignity and their honor.

Al Qaeda, 24 April 2002.

Then came the September 11th blessed operation to support this promise [support the jihad in Palestine]. The attack was against the World Trade Center, the largest financial center supporting the Jews. The Pentagon was the main source of the Jewish military machine on one hand, and its main supporter, on the other.

Al Qaeda, 26 April 2002.

We still are at the beginning of the way. The Americans have still not tasted from our hands what we have tasted from theirs. The [number of] killed in the World Trade Center and the Pentagon were no more than fair exchange for the ones killed in the al-Amiriya shelter in Iraq, and are but a tiny part of the exchange for those killed in Palestine, Somalia, Sudan, the Philippines, Bosnia, Kashmir, Chechnya and Afghanistan.

Sulaiman Abu Ghaith, 12 June 2002.

My work is a message…to the infidels that you should leave the Arabian Peninsula defeated and stop giving a hand to help the coward Jews in Palestine. Allah may reward all those who trained me on this path and were behind this noble act, and a special mention should be made of the Mujahid leader Sheikh Osama bin Laden, may Allah protect him.

Abdulaziz al-Omari. 9/11 hijacker, 10 September 2002.

It seems that the beasts of the White House have forgotten one very important fact—and we are very proud to note it—Al Qaeda. This is the organization that terrorized the core of the infidel West, and made from several youngsters, who owned nothing but love for Allah and his messenger, a means to punish the sons of the bitches. Moreover, these youngsters demonstrated the finest example of leaving the materialist life. They could enjoy the good life, yet they ran away from it, wishing only what Allah could give them. They sold their souls to Allah, and he accepted them.

Abu Shihab al-Qandahari, 26 December 2002.

On that blessed Tuesday [September 11th, 2001]…They [hijackers] smashed the American idols and damaged its very heart, the Pentagon. They struck the very heart of the American economy, rubbed America's nose in the dirt, and dragged its pride through the mud. The Towers of New York collapsed, and their collapse precipitated an even greater debacle: the collapse of the myth of America the great power and the collapse of the myth of democracy; people began to understand that American values could sink no lower. The myth of the land of freedom was destroyed; the myth of American national security was smashed; and the myth of the CIA collapsed... People discovered that it was possible to strike at America, that oppressive power, and that it was possible to humiliate it, to bring it into contempt and to defeat it.

Osama bin Laden, 11 February 2003.

America is the enemy that every Muslim should fight. There is no way the Arab nation can be saved except through jihad...I tell you our battle with you will continue...We will erase the shame [inflicted on Arabs] with our hands and all our force...The only solution is for them [Americans] to leave the lands of the Muslims...Martyrdom attacks heal the hearts of Muslims, and have a moral and material impact...These attacks break their [Americans'] hearts and destroy their morale.

Saeed al-Ghamdi, 9/11 hijacker, 10 September 2003.

We never imagined that the Commander-in-Chief of the American Armed Forces would abandon 50,000 of his citizens in the Twin Towers to face this great horror alone when they needed him most. It seemed to him that a girl's story about her goat and its butting was more important than dealing with planes and their 'butting' into skyscrapers. This allowed us three times the amount of time needed for the operations, Allah be praised.

Osama bin Laden, 29 October 2004.

SEX TRADE

You [the United States] are a nation that practices the trade of sex in all its forms, directly and indirectly. Giant corporations and establishments are established on this under the name of art, entertainment, tourism and freedom.

Al Qaeda, 24 November 2002.

SHI'ITE MUSLIMS

The danger of the Shi'ites to the region is no less than that posed by the Jews and the Christians. Throughout Islamic history, the Shi'ites helped the Christians and the polytheists in their battles against Muslim countries. The seemingly anti-Jewish and anti-Christian Shi'ite hatred is nothing but slogans used to export the Khomeini revolution... We witnessed how the Shi'ite clergy in Iraq rushed to open the gates for the Crusaders, and how they cooperated with them in order to control Iraq.

Al Qaeda, 25 April 2003.

We are hereby threatening all the Shi'ites...for being the knife that is stabbing [betraying] this Muslim community, for what you have done in support of the Crusader occupation in the Land of the Two Rivers...for your collaboration with the occupiers.

The Military Committee of Abu Anas al-Shami Brigade, 9 December 2004.

The brothers in Mesopotamia certainly know that targeting the mayors, representatives of local municipalities, and the Shi'ite dogs sometimes have a greater effect than attacking the Americans.

Abu Yassef Sayyaf, 8 January 2005.

What harvest have the American aggressors and their Shi'ite allies reaped from the invasion of and aggression against the peaceful lands of Islam? Their outrages and blatant lies have become apparent to the entire world, and their arguments and false claims of achieving security and safety for the apostate Iraqi government have all collapsed.

Abu Mus'ab al-Zarqawi, 23 January 2005.

They [Crusaders] came and spread mischief and oppression, violated Muslim sacred symbols, spread their infidel system, and transgressed all bounds against Muslim honor and dignity. They were and still are being aided by their allies from the Shi'ites. The Shi'ite sect has always spearheaded any war against Islam and Muslims throughout history.

Abu Mus'ab al-Zarqawi, 18 May 2005.

SOCIALISTS

Socialists are infidels wherever they are, whether they are in Baghdad or Aden.

Osama bin Laden, 19 January 2003.

SOMALIA (1993-1994)

But your most disgraceful case was in Somalia...when tens of your soldiers were killed in minor battles and one American pilot was dragged in the streets of Mogadishu, you left the area carrying disappointment, humiliation, defeat and your dead with you. Clinton appeared in front of the whole world threatening and promising revenge, but these threats were merely a preparation for withdrawal...the extent of your impotence and weaknesses became very clear.

Osama bin Laden, 23 August 1996.

Resistance started against the American invasion because Muslims did not believe the U.S. allegations that they came to save the Somalis...Muslims over there cooperated with some Arab Mujahideen who were in Afghanistan. They participated with their brothers in Somalia against the American occupation troops and killed large numbers of them... After a little resistance, the American troops left after achieving nothing.

They left after claiming that they were the largest power on earth. They left after some resistance from powerless, poor, unarmed people whose only weapon is the belief in Allah the Almighty, and who do not fear the fabricated American media lies.

Osama bin Laden, March 1997.

The United States alleges that I am fully responsible for the killing of its soldiers in Somalia. Allah knows that we have been pleased at the killing of American soldiers in Somalia. This was achieved by the grace of Allah and the efforts of the Mujahideen from among the Somali brothers and other Arab Mujahideen who had been in Afghanistan before that.

Osama bin Laden, 22 December 1998.

We think that the United States is very much weaker than Russia. Based on the reports we received from our brothers who participated in jihad in Somalia, we learned that they saw the weakness, frailty and cowardice of U.S. troops. Only 80 US troops were killed. Nonetheless, they fled in the heart of darkness, frustrated, after they had caused great commotion about the New World Order.

Osama bin Laden, 10 June 1999.

There was a huge aura over America—the United States—that terrified people even before they entered combat. Our brothers who were here in Afghanistan tested them, and together with some of the Mujahideen in Somalia, Allah granted them victory. America existed dragging its tails in failure, defeat and ruin, caring for nothing.

Osama bin Laden, 21 October 2001.

They [the men of Al Qaeda] offered the Somalis ten thousand dollars for each American soldier that they would kidnap. This, in their attempt to lure the American forces in[to] the Somali swamp for as extended a period as possible, so that it would be possible to deplete them and then annihilate them inside it, as was done to the Soviet Union in Afghanistan.

Salim al-Makhi, "Mending the Hearts of the Believers." October/November 2002.

Later, after the Second Gulf War, the Americans sent their forces into Somalia, where they killed thirteen thousand Somalis...Then the lions of Islam awoke among the Afghan Arabs, and they came to the aid [of the Somalis] and, together with their brothers in that country, they dragged America's pride through the mud. They killed them; they destroyed their tanks and brought down their planes. America and her allies fled under cover of night, each avoiding looking at the other. Praise and thanks be to Allah!

Osama bin Laden, 11 February 2003.

SOUTH/SOUTHEAST ASIA

The human strategic depth of the Muslims is in our brothers in Indonesia, Malaysia, Bangladesh, Pakistan and India, and the Muslim community must take them into account...we must translate our jihad culture to them.

Salim al-Makhi, "Mending the Hearts of the Believers." October/November, 2002.

Our intention is to establish an Islamic country in Southeast Asia. As to how we will achieve it, we have our plans, but we are not going to divulge them.

Bobby Mahmud, 21 August 2003.

SPAIN

Therefore we say that, in order to force the Spanish government to withdraw from Iraq, the resistance should deal painful blows to its forces. This should be accompanied by an information campaign clarifying the truth of the matter inside Iraq. It is necessary to make utmost use of the upcoming general election in Spain in March 2004...We think that the Spanish government could not tolerate more than two, maximum three blows, after which it will have to withdraw as a result of popular pressure. If its troops still remain in Iraq after these blows, then the victory of the Socialist Party is almost secured, and the withdrawal of the Spanish forces will be on its electoral program.

Sheikh Yousef al-Ayiri, 10 December 2003.

STRATEGY

America will be mistaken if it thinks that Osama bin Laden can fight such a great country. But Osama bin Laden is confident that, by the grace of Allah, praise and glory be to Him, the Muslim community will carry out this duty.

Osama bin Laden, 22 December 1998.

In our opinion, America has entered the phase of the beginning of the end. America is talking about wanting to uproot terrorism in Afghanistan, but the truth is that those in Afghanistan have succeeded in uprooting America from its fortresses and bases, and have dragged it, humiliated and shame-faced, to Afghanistan, where their hands, bayonets, and weapons can reach her. America lost even before it entered into battle.

Mahfouz Walad al-Walid, 30 November 2001.

We must seek to move the battlefront to the heart of the Islamic world, which represents the true arena of the battle and the theater of the major battles in defense of Islam.

Ayman al-Zawahiri, 2 December 2001.

We believe we are still at the beginning of this war...So if we are killed or captured or the enemies of Allah manage to achieve one victory...we should not forget that this path is long, and it is a path that the Muslims have to walk upon until Judgment Day.

Sulaiman Abu Ghaith, January 2002.

It appears, therefore, that the imbalance between America and the Mujahideen, of which the cowards [clerics] speak, is exactly what is needed to confront the Western military machine, particularly the American [machine]. [America] is baffled by fourth-generation warfare that suits the jihad avant-garde—especially at a time when the Islamic peoples have re-espoused jihad, after they had nothing left to lose because of the humiliation that is their daily lot.

Abu Ubayd al-Qurashi, January/February 2002.

Sheikh Osama bin Laden thinks of America as a big cancer and a snake that is causing all the humiliations Islam is going through today. He sees America as a strategic target that will lead to victory in Palestine and in all the other lands of Islam. Striking the Americans is similar to directly striking all the tyrants who are behaving arrogantly on all the Muslims in the world.

Abdul Adheem al-Muhajir, 2 May 2002.

It is enough to have a few hundred strong fighters to drive crazy the mightiest, best trained and best armed armies. With Allah's help this is what is happening.

Sayf al-Ansari, 18 September 2002.

Al Qaeda [planned] with premeditation [to carry out] a new enticement plan in Afghanistan: To strike at the Americans directly and deal a blow to the three main pillars of the administration [policy, economy and military power] in order to achieve some important goals, with none more supreme:

To banish the idol-worshippers from the Saudi Arabian Peninsula and raise the banner of the liberation of the Muslim holy sites—from the Jews and the Americans. To call the Muslim youth worldwide to rally around the banner, in order to train them in weapons and various methods of combat and the thought patterns behind them, and to set up cells throughout the world.

To introduce the Muslim community to the true face of its enemy—the Jews and the Crusaders—and to the fact that the struggle against them is eternal...To divide the ranks of the Muslim community into two separate camps: faith and heresy... To expose before the Muslim community the vulnerabilities of its foe, the means to strike it a blow and deplete it, and the ways to annihilate it—both in its own territory and in our deserts.

To remove the American fear from the heart of the entire world...To lure the American forces into an unequal campaign, in order to deplete the enemy's resources and ruin it—according to the same pattern as its Russian predecessor. To initiate a struggle between the American forces and the people of the Muslim community (but not the armies of the rulers) in the framework of an ongoing campaign without boundaries, that will begin in the United States and spread from Afghanistan to Mauritania...

The Americans have indeed swallowed the bait and have fallen in our trap, and Al Qaeda has succeeded in its plans: Thus the first stage in the plans of Al Qaeda has been completed... Soon another stage will begin, of which the vanguard force and the Muslim community will be a part, against the Jews and the Americans...And have we purchased weapons and prepared ammunition for the jihad on behalf of Allah.

Salim al-Makhi, "The Master Trap." October/November 2002.

In its war with America, Al Qaeda adopted the strategy of expanding the battle area...This strategy has priceless advantages; the enemy, who had only his country to defend, realized that he now must defend his enormous interests in every country... While this strategy might cause some damages to Muslims in the process of defending the Muslim community, this happens all the time, and in every jihad.

Al Qaeda in Saudi Arabia, 3 September 2003.

[At the] Management of Barbarism phase, [the Mujahideen are to] established internal security, ensure food and medical supplies, defend the zone from external attack, establish Shari'a justice, an armed force, an intelligence service, provide economic sufficiency, defend against [public] hypocrisy and deviant opinions and ensure obedience, and the establishment of alliances with neighboring elements that are yet to give total conformity to the Management, and improve management structures.

Abu Bakr Naji, 2 March 2005.

[September 11 attacks] destroyed the peoples' awe of America and of the lesser ranking apostate armies...caused the U.S. to lose its grandeur and were planned to force the United States into the trap of revenge by invading Afghanistan and coming face to face with the people of the occupied lands.

Abu Bakr Naji, 2 March 2005.

SUDAN

[In response to claims he has training camps in Sudan]: The rubbish of the media and the embassies. I am a construction engineer and an agriculturalist. If I had training camps here in Sudan, I couldn't possibly do this job.

Osama bin Laden, 6 December 1993.

SUPERPOWERS, MYTH OF THE

But by the grace of Allah, a safe base is now available in the high Hindu Kush Mountains in Khurasan; where—by the grace of Allah—the largest infidel military force of the world [U.S.S.R.] was destroyed. And the myth of the superpower withered in front of the Mujahideen cries of Allah is the greatest.

Osama bin Laden, 23 August 1996.

So our experience in this jihad [War against the U.S.S.R. in Afghanistan] was great, by the grace of Allah, praise and glory be to Him. The greatest benefit to us was that the myth of the superpower was destroyed, not only in my mind but also in the minds of all Muslims.

Osama bin Laden, March 1997.

After Allah honored us with victory in Afghanistan, and justice prevailed and the killing of those who slaughtered millions of Muslims in the Muslim republics, it cleared from Muslim minds the myth of the superpowers.

Osama bin Laden, 28 May 1998.

SYRIA

[Concerning the assassination of former Lebanese Prime Minister Rafiq al-Hariri]

The priorities of the Al Qaeda Organization in Syria are focused on its foundation [in the country], not on blowing up cars in towns.

1) Our main priorities are now aiding our brothers in Iraq and Palestine.

2) The way we support our brothers in the Arabian Peninsula has never been and will never be by way of what has happened today.

3) What Al Qaeda carried out in New York and Washington and the sacrifices it made of its finest men were on behalf of Beirut; it is illogical that it would today carry out bombings against Beirut's streets and buildings.

Al Qaeda Organization in Greater Syria, 14 February 2005.

TACTICS

Preparations for major operations take a certain amount of time, unlike minor operations. If we wanted small actions, the matter would have easily been carried out immediately after the [August 1996] statement. [But] the nature of the battle calls for operations of a specific type that will make an impact on the enemy, and this calls for excellent preparations.

Osama bin Laden, 27 November 1996.

Choosing the Targets and Concentrating on the Martyrdom Operations:

I. Changing the method of strikes: The Mujahid Islamic movement must escalate its methods of strikes and tools of resisting the enemies to keep up with the tremendous increase in the number of its enemies, the quality of their weapons, their destructive powers, their disregard for all taboos, and disrespect for the customs of wars and conflicts.

In this regard, we concentrate on the following:

(1). The need to inflict the maximum casualties against the opponent, for this is the language understood by the West, no matter how much time and effort such operations take.

(2). The need to concentrate on the method of martyrdom operations as the most successful way of inflicting damage against the opponent and the least costly to the Mujahideen in terms of casualties.

(3). The targets as well as the type and method of weapons used must be chosen to have an impact on the structure of the enemy and deter it enough to stop its brutality, arrogance and disregard for all taboos and customs. It must restore the struggle to its real size.

(4). To re-emphasize what we have already explained, we reiterate that focusing on the domestic enemy alone will not be feasible at this stage.

Ayman al-Zawahiri, 2 December 2001.

Killing them with a single bullet, a stab, or device made up of a popular mix of explosives or hitting them with an iron rod is not impossible. Burning down their property with Molotov cocktails is not difficult. With the available means, small groups could prove to be a frightening horror for the Americans and the Jews.

Ayman al-Zawahiri, 2 December 2001.

There must be plans in place for hitting buildings with high human intensity like skyscrapers, ports, airports, nuclear power plants and places where large numbers of people gather like football grounds.

Manual of Afghan Jihad, 2 February 2002.

The security, military, and political necessities require that the Mujahideen undertake some actions that might seem negative to absorb the power of the enemy, exhaust it more, involve it in a war of attrition, protect the positions and the Mujahideen, and keep the cause alive. Such behavior I considered part of the interim tasks, and it aims to deter the aggression as part of maintaining a realistic and strategic balance.

Abu Ayman al-Hilali, 15 March 2002.

The hunt for the enemy who is represented in the Crusader-Jewish Alliance by the weapon of [spreading] fear... is an effective weapon which must be used against the enemy by widening the front lines and carrying out focused and quick operations against his body, which is spread over a large area in this world, so that he shall feel threatened, insecure and instable on the land, sea and in the air.

Sulaiman Abu Ghaith, 7 December 2002.

Targets inside the cities are considered a sort of military diplomacy. Normally, this kind of diplomacy is written in blood and decorated with body parts and the smell of guns. It carries a political meaning that relates to the nature of the faith's struggle. The intent is to send messages to different directions.

Abdul Aziz al-Muqrin, 29 March 2004.

TALIBAN

We were in deep grief during the dispute between these factions and the parties of the Mujahideen. But Allah Almighty was gracious to the Arab nations by giving them the Taliban movement, which came to rescue this jihad from the U.S. scheme...to form a secular government...It [the Taliban] was not a force being pushed in from abroad, as the Crusaders in the Western media try to depict them; but it was rather a pulling force from the inside. People had become sick and tired of road bandits and from paying taxes and protection money... because of the popular support, after the people had reached a state of despair from previous events, they were successful.

Osama bin Laden, 10 June 1999.

I have a spiritual relationship with Mullah Omar. He is a great and brave Muslim of this age. He does not fear anyone but Allah. He is not under any personal relationship or obligation to me. He is only discharging his religious duty. I, too, have not chosen this life out of any personal consideration.

Osama bin Laden, 7 November 2001.

I support the Taliban for several reasons. First, because support for it is support for the truth. We are Muslims, preaching the truth; we are commanded to make the truth prevail…I would not be exaggerating if I said that today there is no regime on the face of the earth that rules according to Islam…except the Islamic Emirate ruled by the Taliban.

Mahfouz Walad al-Walid, 30 November 2001.

TERRORISM

We also have been hit with some of the traces of this [American] campaign [against the Muslim world] as we were accused of funding terrorism, and being members of an international terrorist organization. Their aims in making these allegations were to place psychological pressure on the Mujahideen and their supporters so that they would forsake the obligation of jihad and the resistance of oppression and American-Israeli occupation of Islamic sacred lands…As for their accusations of terrorizing the innocent, the children, and the women, these are in the category 'accusing others with their own affliction in order to fool the masses.' The evidence overwhelmingly shows America and Israel killing the weaker men, women, and children in the Muslim world and elsewhere.

Osama bin Laden, October/November 1996.

The U.S. today...has set a double standard, calling whoever goes against its injustice a terrorist. It wants to occupy our countries, steal our resources, impose on us agents to rule us based not on what Allah has revealed, and wants us to agree on all these. If we refuse to do so, it will say you are terrorists... Wherever we look, we find the U.S. as the leader of terrorism and crime in the world...The U.S. does not consider it terrorism when hundreds of thousands of our sons and brothers in Iraq died for lack of food or medicine.

Osama bin Laden, March 1997.

Besides, terrorism can be commendable, and it can be reprehensible. Terrifying an innocent person and terrorizing him is objectionable and unjust...Whereas, terrorizing oppressors and criminals and thieves and robbers is necessary for the safety of people and for the protection of their property...Every state and every civilization and culture has to resort to terrorism under certain circumstances for the purpose of abolishing tyranny and corruption...The terrorism we practice is of the commendable kind, for it is directed at the tyrants and the aggressors and the enemies of Allah, the tyrants, the traitors who commit acts of treason against their own countries and their own faith and their own Prophet and their own nation.

Osama bin Laden, 28 May 1998.

Let us say that there are two parties to the conflict: the first party is world Christianity, which is allied with Zionist Jewry and led by the United States, Britain, and Israel; while the second party is the Muslim world. In such a conflict, it is unacceptable to see the first party mount attacks, desecrate lands and holy shrines, and plunder the Muslims' oil. When it is met by any resistance on the part of the Muslims, this party brands the Muslims as terrorists...We believe that it is our religious duty to resist this occupation with all the power that we have and to punish it using the same means it is pursuing us with.

Osama bin Laden, 10 June 1999.

Americans, Indians and Russians are the leading terrorists...While the people of Afghanistan, Kashmir and Chechnya are dying of hunger, Americans celebrate Christmas. How is it possible? The Mujahideen will continue their efforts against Americans, Russians and Indians...Islam will spread over the entire world.

Nazeer Ahmed Mujjaid, 21 December 1999.

The Muslim community must also know that the U.S. version of terrorism is a kind of deception. Is it logical for the United States and its allies to carry out this repression, persecution, plundering, and bloodletting over these long years without this being called terrorism, while when the victim tries to seek justice, he is described as terrorist?

Sulaiman Abu Ghaith, 9 October 2001.

Just as they're killing us, we have to kill them so that there will be a balance of terror. This is the first time the balance of terror has been close between the two parties, between Muslims and Americans, in the modern age. American politicians used to do whatever they wanted with us. The victim was forbidden to scream or to moan.

Osama bin Laden, 21 October 2001.

Not all terrorism is cursed; some terrorism is blessed. A thief, a criminal, for example, feels terrorized by the police. So, do we say to the policeman, "You are a terrorist?" No. Police terrorism against criminals is a blessed terrorism because it will prevent the criminal from repeating his deed. America and Israel exercise the condemned terrorism. We practice the good terrorism which stops them from killing our children in Palestine and elsewhere.

Osama bin Laden, 21 October 2001.

What can those who allege that this is a war against terrorism say? What terrorism are they speaking about at a time when the Muslim community has been slaughtered for tens of years without hearing their voices, without seeing any action by them? But when the victim starts to take revenge for those innocent children in Palestine, Iraq, southern Sudan, Somalia, Kashmir and the Philippines, the rulers' Islamic clerics and the hypocrites come to defend the clear blasphemy.

Osama bin Laden, 3 November 2001.

The United States is practicing the detestable terrorism in its ugliest forms in Palestine and Iraq.

Osama bin Laden, 26 December 2001.

So does 'terrorist' mean somebody who defends his religion, his country and his dead and injured people?!!! Is this a terrorist act? Yes, it is 'terrorist' according to the American point of view only because we are resisting the Americans and refusing their imperialism. There is no terrorism in Islam, and we do not consider the right of the people to resist as 'terrorism', neither according to our religion nor any other religion.

Taliban Military Commander, 2 April 2002.

THAILAND

Their capital [Bangkok] will be burned down in the same way the Patani capital has been burned...we pledge before Allah that from now on, the infidel will suffer sleepless nights.

We advise you to cancel your trip to Thailand if you do not want to take risks...we advise you to avoid police stations, music concerts, cafes, bars, nightclubs, railway stations and airports...Be informed that the coming operations are targeting Thai policemen and soldiers only. The operations will be performed by Patani liberation movements that are not under our control. Therefore, we are not responsible for damages or loss after this warning.

Patani United Liberation Organization, October 2004.

TORTURE

Security personnel in our countries arrest brothers and obtain the needed information through interrogation and torture. The Military Organization must do likewise... Information is collected in this method by kidnapping an enemy individual, interrogating him and torturing him. This source of information is not permanent.

Al Qaeda, 10 May 2000.

TURKEY

I accept that I am an Al Qaeda warrior...Even if Osama dies, our jihad will continue. Al Qaeda exists in all of the Islamic world for victory, and until this fight is finished with success, it will continue...[If Turkey supports U.S. policy] we will never leave the Republic of Turkey, the price will be paid. The war is not over and it will continue until imperialist forces withdraw.

Harun Ilhan, 13 September 2004.

We cannot speak of an Al Qaeda branch in Turkey—but there are ties of mutual assistance.

Adnan Ersoz, 13 September 2004.

UNITED NATIONS

The United Nations' insistence to convict the victims and support the aggressors constitutes a serious precedent which shows the extent of injustice that has been allowed to take root in this land.

Osama bin Laden, 28 May 1998.

Some 13,000 from among our brothers, women, and sons in Somalia were killed under the banner of the United Nations.

Reports, corroborated by photographs, said that our Somali brothers were grilled as if they were sheep.

Osama bin Laden, 10 June 1999.

For several years our brothers have been killed, our women have been raped, and our children have been massacred in the safe havens of the United Nations and with its knowledge and cooperation. Those who refer our tragedies today to the United Nations, so that they can be resolved, are hypocrites who deceive Allah, His Prophet and the believers. Are not our tragedies but caused by the United Nations? Who issued the Partition Resolution on Palestine in 1947 and surrendered the land of Muslims to the Jews? It was the United Nations in its resolution in 1947...This is the United Nations from which we have suffered greatly. Under no circumstances should any Muslim or sane person resort to the United Nations. The United Nations is nothing but a tool of crime. We are being massacred everyday, while the United Nations continues to sit idly by.

Osama bin Laden, 3 November 2001.

The talk about the United Nations as an independent party ruling the world is nonsense. Perhaps the United Nations was a body whose judgment was sought and accepted by the nations that established it, including the United States. However, today it is a toy in the hands of World Zionism. The United States ignored the United Nations when it shyly opposed its invasion of Iraq. Three Crusader countries officially participated in the war with it, disregarding the U.N. resolutions.

Al Qaeda in Saudi Arabia, 3 September 2003.

As for President Bush, the leaders who are revolving in his orbit, the leading media companies, and the United Nations, which makes laws for relations between the masters of veto and the slaves of the General Assembly, these are only some of the tools used to deceive and exploit peoples.

Osama bin Laden, 15 April 2004

And as for the United Nations, it is nothing but an instrument of the Zionist Crusade hiding behind works of charity.

Osama bin Laden, 6 May 2004.

UNITED STATES

The coming days will prove that America will share the fate of the U.S.S.R.: it will be struck from all sides.

World Islamic Front for Jihad against the Jews and Crusaders, 12 August 1998.

The American imposes himself on everyone. Americans accuse our children in Palestine of being terrorists—those children, who have no weapons and have not even reached maturity. At the same time, Americans defend a country, the state of the Jews, that has a policy to destroy the future of these children. We are sure of our victory against the Americans and the Jews as promised by the Prophet...Also, by the testimony of relief workers in Iraq, the American-led sanctions resulted in the death of more than one million Iraqi children. All of this is done in the name of American interests. We believe that the biggest thieves in the world and the terrorists are the Americans. The only way for us to fend off these assaults is to use similar means.

Osama bin Laden, February 1999.

The current situation in Afghanistan is related to a bigger cause—that is the destruction of America...This is not a matter of weapons. We are hopeful for Allah's help. The real matter is the extinction of America. And, Allah willing, it [America] will fall to the ground.

Mullah Omar, 15 November 2001.

America, with the collaboration of the Jews, is the leader of corruption and the breakdown [of values], whether moral, ideological, political or economic corruption. It disseminates abomination and licentiousness among the people via the cheap media and the vile curricula.

Sulaiman Abu Ghaith, 12 June 2002.

In any event, may the United States sink in the darkness of confusion and illusion, anchored in the depths of fear and the corridors of horror with its odd mentality, continue crippled on its way, dig its own grave, and flounder in the depths of hell—because Al Qaeda has succeeded in fooling them and has cast upon them its cloak of execution, may it [Al Qaeda] expel the Jews and their Crusader offspring.

Salim al-Makhi, "Mending the Hearts of the Believers." October/November 2002.

What you [the United States] have suffered until now are only the initial skirmishes... The real battle has not started yet...We do not expect justice, fairness or compliance with morals, principles or creeds from America. It has set to the world an example in contempt for principles, including those in agreements it signed.

Ayman al-Zawahiri, 3 August 2003.

UNITED STATES—ARMED FORCES

We learned from those who fought there [Somalia, October 1993], that they were surprised to see the low spiritual morale of the American fighters in comparison with the experience they had with the Russian fighters. The Americans ran away from those fighters who fought and killed them, while the latter were still there.

Osama bin Laden, March 1997.

The youth were surprised at the low morale of the American soldiers and realized more than before that the American soldiers are paper tigers. After a few blows [in Somalia, 1993-1994], they ran in defeat and America forgot about all the hoopla and media propaganda...about being the world leader, and the leader of the New World Order. After a few blows, they forgot about this title and left, dragging their corpses and their shameful defeat and stopped using such titles.

Osama bin Laden, 28 May 1998.

The raid [Clinton administration missile attacks in response to Al Qaeda bombings of U.S. embassies in Kenya and Tanzania—August 1898) has also proven that the American army is going down hill in its morale. Its members are too cowardly and too fearful to meet the young people of Islam face to face.

Osama bin Laden, 22 December 1998.

The American forces should expect reactions to their actions, from the Muslim world. Any thief or criminal or robber who enters the countries of others in order to steal should expect to be exposed to murder at any time...The American forces should expect reactions from the Muslim world which are proportionate to the injustice these forces inflict.

Osama bin Laden, 22 December 1998.

We have realized from our defense and fighting against the American enemy that, in combat, they mainly depend on psychological warfare. This is in light of the huge media machine they have. They also depend on massive air strikes so as to conceal their most prominent point of weakness, which is the fear, cowardliness, and the absence of combat spirit among U.S. soldiers. Those soldiers are completely convinced of the injustice and lying of their government. They also lack a fair cause to defend. They only fight for capitalists, usury takers, and the merchants of arms and oil, including the gang of crime at the White House. This is in addition to Crusader and personal grudges by Bush the father.

Osama bin Laden, 19 January 2003.

Oh people, do not fear America and its army. By Allah, we have struck them time and time again, and they have been defeated time after time. In combat they are the most cowardly of people. Our defense and our war against the American enemy have shown that [America's] warfare is mainly psychological in nature, because of the vast propaganda apparatus at its disposal. It is also based upon intensive bombing from the air, which is designed to conceal its most obvious weakness: cowardice and the American soldier's lack of fighting spirit.

Osama bin Laden, 11 February 2003.

The American soldier is not fit for combat. This is the truth that the leaders of the Pentagon know, as much as we and everyone who was engaged with them know. The Hollywood promotions will not succeed in the real battlefield. Therefore, the American commanders tend to use the air force and missile bombardment to vacate the ground from any resistance, paving the way for the advance of the American phonies.

Saif al-Adel, March 2003.

[I have a] message to the American soldiers: For the American soldiers, we say you have to know that your government has become a big evil, killing innocent people, destroying homes, stealing our money and holding our sons in jail. We promise that we will not let you live safely, and you will not see from us anything else—just bombs, fire, destroying homes, cutting your heads. Our Mujahideen is coming to you very soon to let you see what you didn't see before.

Hazem al-Kashmiri, 17 October 2003.

The Americans have become weaker in Iraq. Their soldiers are cowards because they have no faith in their leaders.

Ayman al-Zawahiri, 19 December 2003.

UNITED STATES—FOREIGN POLICY

Despite the continuing American occupation of the Land of the Two Holy Mosques, America continues to claim that it is upholding the banner of freedom and humanity, whilst these deeds which they did, you would find that the most ravenous of animals would not descend to.

Osama bin Laden, October/November 1996.

But I say if the American government is serious about avoiding the explosions inside the U.S., then let it stop provoking the feelings of 1,250 million Muslims. Those hundreds of thousands who have been killed or displaced in Iraq, Palestine, Lebanon, do have brothers and relatives...The U.S. will drive them to transfer the battle into the United States. Everything is made possible to protect the blood of the American citizen while the bloodshed of Muslims is allowed in every place. With this kind of behavior, the U.S. government is hurting itself, hurting Muslims and hurting the American people.

Osama bin Laden, March 1997.

America controls the governments of the Islamic countries. The people ask to follow Islam, but the governments do not listen because they are in the grip of the United States. If someone follows the path of Islam, the government arrests him, tortures him or kills him. This is the doing of America. If it stops supporting those governments and lets the people deal with them, then such things won't happen. America has created the evil that is attacking it. The evil will not disappear even if I die and Osama dies and others die. The U.S. should step back and review its policy. It should stop trying to impose its empire on the rest of the world, especially on Islamic countries.

Mullah Omar, 21 September 2001.

Members of the U.S. administration know that when Al Qaeda promises, it delivers, and the information is what we see not what we hear. The storm of airplanes will not be calmed, if it is Allah's will. The storm will not calm, especially as long as you do not end your support for the Jews in Palestine, lift your embargo from around the Iraqi people and have left the Arabian Peninsula, and stop your support of the Hindus against the Muslims in Kashmir.

Sulaiman Abu Ghaith, 13 October 2001.

Truly, America is not, nor has it ever been, a land of treaty or alliance. If we were to line up with the other side and say that it is a land of peace, we would say that it has turned into a land of war. That occurred with its violation of the treaty and its help to the Jews for more than fifty years in occupying Palestine, banishing its people and killing them. It is a land of war that violated its treaty when it attacked and blockaded Iraq, attacked and blockaded Sudan, attacked and blockaded Afghanistan. It has oppressed Muslims in every place for decades and has openly supported their enemies against them.

Al Qaeda, 24 April 2002.

UNITED STATES—JIHAD AGAINST THE

We declared jihad against the U.S. government, because the U.S. government is unjust, criminal and tyrannical. It has committed acts that are extremely unjust, hideous and criminal, whether directly or through its support of the Israeli occupation of the Prophet's Night Travel Land [Palestine]. And we believe the U.S. is directly responsible for those who were killed in Palestine, Lebanon and Iraq...This U.S. government abandoned even humanitarian feelings by these hideous crimes...For this and other acts of aggression and injustice, we have declared jihad against the U S

Osama bin Laden, March 1997.

The call to wage war against America was made because America has spear-headed the Crusade against the Muslim community, sending tens of thousands of its troops to the Land of the Two Holy Mosques, over and above its meddling in its affairs and its politics, and its support of the oppressive, corrupt and tyrannical regime that is in control. These are the reasons behind the singling out of America as a target. And not exempt of responsibility are those Western regimes whose presence in the region offers support to the American troops there.

Osama bin Laden, 28 May 1998.

Why are we fighting and opposing you? The answer is very simple: Because you attacked us and continue to attack us. You attacked us in Palestine...You attacked us in Somalia; you supported the Russian atrocities against us in Chechnya, the Indian oppression against us in Kashmir, and the Jewish aggression against us in Lebanon. Under your supervision, consent and orders, the governments of our countries, which act as your agents, attack us on a daily basis. These governments prevent our people from establishing the Shari'a, using violence and lies to do so...

These governments steal our Muslim community's wealth and sell them to you at a paltry price. These governments have surrendered to the Jews, and handed them most of Palestine, acknowledging the existence of their state over the dismembered limbs of their own people...Your forces occupy our countries; you spread your military bases throughout them; you corrupt our lands, and you besiege our sanctities, to protect the security of the Jews and to ensure the continuity of your pillage of our treasures.

Al Qaeda, 24 November 2002.

UNITED STATES—STRATEGY

The Bush-Blair agreement pretends that it wants to put an end to terrorism. However, it is no longer a secret, even from the masses, that it wants to put an end to Islam...Nor is it a secret that the preparations underway at present for an attack upon Iraq are but one link in a chain of attacks—in preparation—on the countries of the region, including Syria,

Iran, Egypt and Sudan. However, the preparations for the division of the Land of the Two Holy Mosques constitute the main part of their plan. This, we know, is a long-standing strategic aim [which has existed] every since [Saudi Arabia] transferred its dependence from Great Britain to the United States six decades ago.

Osama bin Laden, 11 February 2003.

After dividing Iraq, Saudi Arabia, Iran, Syria, and Pakistan will come next. They would leave around Israel only dismembered semi-states that are subservient to the United States and Israel.

Ayman al-Zawahiri, 21 May 2003.

The Crusader campaign, which is led by the United States, supported by its infidel and hypocrite allies and supporters, is intended against Islam and Muslims, even if it claims that it is fighting terrorism, for it is what we call jihad.

Ayman al-Zawahiri, 28 September 2003.

UZBEKISTAN

On 13/6/1425 (7/30/04), a number of Muslim youth carried out martyrdom operations that terrorized the apostate [Uzbek] government and her infidel allies from the Americans and the Jews...These martyrdom operations...will not stop...

and this is a response to the injustice of the apostate [Uzbek] government and an effort to support the jihad of our Muslim brothers in Iraq, Palestine, Afghanistan, the Hijaz [Saudi Arabia], and other Muslim countries that are ruled by the infidels and apostates.

Islamic Jihad Movement in Uzbekistan, 30 July 2004.

Recently, news was received that the Muslim prisoners... were being killed in Uzbekistan and that the number of dead had reached in the thousands...O Muslims! These massacres prove how much the West hates Islam and the Muslims. Although America and Russia compete in Central Asia...when it comes to killing the Muslims, they put their differences aside.

Hizb ut-Tahrir, 21 May 2005.

VICTORY

We are sure of our victory. Our battle with the Americans is larger than our battle with the Russians...We predict a black day for America and the end of the United States, as the United States will be separate states, and will retreat from our land and collect the bodies of its sons back to America, Allah willing.

Osama bin Laden, 28 May 1998.

The movement is driving fast...forward. And I am sure of our victory with Allah's help against America and the Jews. We see this then in the strength of the reaction. Every day the Americans delay their departure, for every day they delay, they will receive a new corpse from Muslim countries.

Osama bin Laden, 28 May 1998.

Allah, who provided us with his support and kept us steadfast until the Soviet Union was defeated, is able to provide us once more with his support to defeat America on the same land and with the same people. We believe that the defeat of America is possible, with the help of Allah, and is even easier for us, Allah permitting, than the defeat of the Soviet Union was before.

Osama bin Laden, 21 October 2001.

It is impossible to win against the people, no matter what the enemy possesses in weaponry, technical capabilities and advanced technology. Victory over the United States is very possible and easy beyond the imagination of many. It has several components; the most important is the elimination of the hypocritical forces fighting on behalf of the American soldier.

Saif al-Adel, March 2003.

[The American] defeat in Iraq and Afghanistan has become just a question of time, Allah willing...[the Americans] are caught between two fires: if they remain there, they will bleed to death, and if they withdraw, they will have lost everything.

Ayman al-Zawahiri, 9 September 2004.

THE WAR AGAINST THE U.S. AND THE WEST

This war will not only be between the people of the Land of the Two Holy Mosques and the Americans, but it will be between the Islamic world and the Americans and their allies, because this war is a new Crusade led by America against the Islamic nations.

Osama bin Laden, November 1996.

I believe that sooner or later the Americans will leave Saudi Arabia and that the war declared by America against the Saudi people means war against all Muslims everywhere. Resistance against America will spread in many, many places in Muslim countries...The solution to this crisis is the withdrawal of American troops...their military presence is an insult for the Saudi people.

Osama bin Laden, 6 December 1996.

In today's wars, there are no morals, and it is clear that mankind has descended to the lowest degree of decadence and oppression. They steal our wealth, our resources and our oil. Our religion is under attack. They kill and murder our brothers. They compromise our honor and our dignity, and dare we utter a single word of protest against the injustice, we are called terrorists. This is compounded injustice.

Osama bin Laden, 28 May 1998.

The World Islamic Front announces that the war has begun. Our response to the barbaric bombardment against the Muslims of Afghanistan and Sudan will be ruthless and violent. All the Islamic world has mobilized to strike a prominent American or Israeli strategic objective, to blow up their airplanes and to seize them.

Osama bin Laden, 24 August 1998.

This battle is not between Al Qaeda and the U.S. This is a battle of Muslims against the global Crusaders...The battle has moved to inside America. We will work to continue this battle, Allah permitting, until victory or until we meet Allah before that occurs.

Osama bin Laden, 21 October 2001.

Here we must note that fighting under such a [Islamic] banner does not necessarily mean that the fighting is free from every blemish and from every error. Fighting may take place under an Islamic banner and yet be marred by violations that impair the perfection of the form demanded in fighting in the way of Allah. However, as long as these violations do not go so far as to affect the nature of the fight, or turn it from its basic direction [the way of Allah], it is difficult for us [Al Qaeda] to deny such a banner the attribute of being Islamic.

Sayf al-Ansari, 14 May 2002.

The incidents that have taken place since the raids of New York and Washington [11 September 2001] until now—like the killing of Germans in Tunisia and the French in Karachi, the bombing of the giant French tanker in Yemen, the killing of Marines in Failaka [in Kuwait], and the British and Australians in the Bali explosions, the recent operation in Moscow, and some sporadic operations here and there—are only reactions and reciprocal actions. These actions were carried out by the zealous sons of Islam in defense of their religion.

Osama bin Laden, 12 November 2002.

You will be killed just as you kill and will be bombed just as you bomb. Expect more that will further distress you. The Muslim community, thanks to Allah, has started to attack you at the hands of its beloved sons, who pledged to Allah to continue jihad, as long as they are alive, through words and weapons to establish right and expose falsehood.

Osama bin Laden, 12 November 2002.

In the year 1418 of the Muslim calendar [1997] the Mujahideen publicly threatened America, [hoping this] would cause it to stop supporting the Jews and to depart the Land of the Two Holy Mosques. The enemy rejected the warning and the Mujahideen managed, through the grace of Allah, to deliver two tremendous blows in East Africa. Later America was warned again, but paid no heed, and Allah sent success to the Mujahideen who, in a tremendous act of self-sacrifice, annihilated the American destroyer *Cole* in Aden. This was a resounding slap in the face for the American military establishment. This operation also revealed the fact that the Yemeni government, like that of the other countries in the region, had collaborated [with the U.S.].

Osama bin Laden, 11 February 2003.

The reasons for war can be divided into two parts:

1). Just wars, waged by a group or people whose will has been plundered and who are repressed and oppressed, against the invading and plundering force or against a tyrant. The goal is to remove the oppression and the aggression and to fight for the sake of Allah in order to impose Shari'a and so that the word of Allah will reign supreme. Examples of this type of fighting are [in] the Land of the Two Holy Mosques, Palestine, Afghanistan, Iraq, Chechnya, Kashmir, the Philippines and so on.

2). Wars of oppression, waged by oppressive forces against

the repressed, with the goal of taking over the beliefs, replacing the religious laws and plundering the resources.

Abu Hajjer, December 2003/January 2004.

The jihad has reached this stage, praise be to Allah, since the successful September 11 operation. The emergence of a number of jihad frontlines in various places around the world, including the regions of Iraq and the Arabian Peninsula, are signs that bode the end of the Crusader and Jewish domination over the Muslim countries and the fall of the apostate regimes that rule Muslim countries.

Al Qaeda's Committee in the Arabian Peninsula, 1 November 2004.

WAR CRIMINALS

The Al Qaeda organization declares that Bush Senior, Bush Junior, Clinton, Blair and Sharon are the arch-criminals from among the Zionists and Crusaders who committed the most heinous actions and atrocities against the Muslim community. They perpetrated murders, torture and displacement. Millions of Muslim men, women and children died without any fault of their own. Al Qaeda stresses that the blood of those killed will not go to waste, Allah willing, until we punish these criminals.

Sulaiman Abu Ghaith, 13 October 2001.

As for the war criminals which you censure and form criminal courts for—you shamelessly ask that your own are granted immunity!! However, history will not forget the war crimes you committed against the Muslims and the rest of the world; those you have killed in Japan, Afghanistan, Somalia, Lebanon and Iraq will remain a shame that you will never be able to escape. It will suffice to remind you of your latest war crimes in Afghanistan, in which densely populated innocent civilian villages were destroyed. Bombs were dropped on mosques causing the roof of the mosque to come crashing down on the heads of the Muslims praying inside. You are the ones who broke the agreement with the Mujahideen when they left Qunduz, bombing them in Jangi fort, and killing more than 1,000 of your prisoners through suffocation and thirst. Allah alone knows how many people have died by torture at the hands of you and your agents. Your planes remain in the Afghan skies, looking for anyone remotely suspicious.

Al Qaeda, 24 November 2002.

WEAPONS OF MASS DESTRUCTION

I would say that acquiring weapons for the defense of Muslims is a religious duty. To seek to possess the weapons that could counter those of the infidels is a religious duty. If I have indeed acquired these weapons, then this is an obligation I carried out and I thank Allah for enabling us to do that. And if I seek to acquire these weapons I am carrying out a duty. It would be a sin for Muslims not to try to possess the weapons that would prevent the infidels from inflicting harm on Muslims. But how we use these weapons, if we possess them, is up to us.

Osama bin Laden, 22 December 1998.

[To Osama bin Laden] Using any biological weapons in self-defense is, in Islam, permissible, and I believe that we are currently operating under a defensive jihad. Obviously, we regret what could happen to innocent people, but there are always people who are war casualties or, if you like, victims of war.

Sheikh Omar bin Bakri Muhammad, May 1999.

I heard the speech of American President Bush yesterday [October 7]. He was scaring the European countries that Osama wanted to attack with weapons of mass destruction. I wish to declare that if America uses chemical or nuclear weapons against us, then we may retort with chemical and nuclear weapons. We have the weapons as a deterrent.

Osama bin Laden, 7 November 2001.

If such a weapon [chemical, biological, or nuclear] is at Al Qaeda's disposal, then it is a deterrent weapon, and not for initiating an action. Let the Americans fear the worst possible scenario when they use any unconventional weapons. We are lying in wait for them.

Mahfouz Walad al-Walid, 30 November 2001.

We have not reached parity with them. We have the right to kill four million Americans—two million of them children—and to exile twice as many and wound and cripple hundreds of thousands. Furthermore, it is our right to fight them with chemical and biological weapons, so as to afflict them with the fatal maladies that have afflicted the Muslims because of the [Americans'] chemical and biological weapons.

Sulaiman Abu Ghaith, 12 June 2002.

Your policy of prohibiting and forcibly removing weapons of mass destruction to ensure world peace is only applied to those countries which you do not permit to possess such weapons. As for the countries you consent to, such as Israel, they are allowed to keep and use such weapons to defend their security. Anyone else who you suspect might be manufacturing or keeping these kinds of weapons, you call them criminals, and you take military action against them.

Al Qaeda, 24 November 2002.

An eye for eye and a tooth for a tooth If the Americans have bombs that no one else owns, Al Qaeda is stronger. It owns 'dirty bombs' and 'lethal viruses bombs,' which could cover the American cities with deadly diseases and turn this nation, which is 'a professional in contempt for other nations,' into a crowd of contaminated and sick people. The coming days will prove that Al Qaeda is capable, with Allah's help, of turning the United States into a lake of lethal radiation, that would seem as the last days of humanity. It would also prove that Al Qaeda is very popular all over the Islamic world.

Abu Shihab al-Qandahari, 26 December 2002.

Anyone who looks at America's acts of aggression against the Muslims and their lands over the recent decades will permit this [the use of WMD] based only on the section of Islamic law called 'Repayment in Kind,' without any need to indicate the other evidence. Some of the brothers have counted the number of Muslims killed with their [America's] direct and indirect weapons, and this number has reached nearly 10 million...If a bomb were dropped on them [the Americans] that would annihilate 10 million and burn their lands to the same extent that they have burned the Muslim lands—this is permissible, with no need to mention any other proof. Yet if we want to annihilate a greater number, we need further evidence.

Sheikh Nasser bin Hamed, 21 May 2003.

Al Qaeda [does not rule out] using Sarin gas and poisoning drinking water in U.S. and Western cities. We will talk about [these weapons] then, and the infidels will know what harms them. They spared no effort in their war on us in Afghanistan. They should not therefore rule out the possibility that we will present them with our capabilities.

Abu Muhammad al-Ablaj, 25 May 2003.

THE WEST

We differentiate between the Western governments and the people of the West. If the people have elected those governments in the latest elections, it is because they have fallen prey to the Western media which portray things contrary to what they really are. And while the slogans raised by those regimes call for humanity, justice, and peace, the behavior of their governments is completely the opposite...

What they ought to do is change their governments which attack our countries. The hostility that America continues to express against the Muslim people has given rise to feelings of animosity on the part of Muslims against America and against the West in general. Those feelings of animosity have produced a change in the behavior of some crushed and subdued groups who, instead of fighting the Americans inside the Muslim countries, went on to fight them inside the United States of America itself. The Western regimes and the government of the United States of America bear the blame for what might happen. If their people do not wish to be harmed inside their very own countries, they should seek to elect governments that are truly representative of them and that can protect their interests

Osama bin Laden, 28 May 1998.

WOMEN

O! you Muslim women, Be aware of extravagance, for it is the enemy of jihad, and it causes the death of the human soul. Beware of the complementary commodities and stick to the basic necessities. Bring up your children to be brave and courageous. Let your houses be places for lions, not chicken farms in which your sons will be fed and then slaughtered by tyrants like sheep. Instill in the hearts of your sons the love for jihad and the love of battlefields. Share the problems of the Muslim community. Live one day a week like refugees and the Mujahideen. They live on dry bread and tea.

Abdullah Azzam, 20 April 1986.

Pledge, O Sister

To the sister believer whose clothes the criminals have stripped off.

To the sister believer whose hair the oppressors have shaved.

To the sister believer whose body has been abused by the human dogs.....

Pledge, O Sister

Covenant, O Sister...to make their women widows and their children orphans.

Covenant, O Sister...to make them desire death and hate appointments and prestige.

Covenant, O Sister...to slaughter them like lambs and let the Nile, al-Asi, and Euphrates Rivers flow with their blood.

Covenant, O Sister...to be a pick of destruction for every godless and apostate regime.

Covenant, O Sister...to retaliate for you against every dog who touches you even with a bad word.

Al Qaeda, 10 May 2000.

O sisters who are following in the footsteps of the virtuous ones by sending their brothers to the arenas of heroism with firmness and their motivation, You are the ones who have incited and motivated, and before then reared all the men who fight the jihad in Palestine, Lebanon, Afghanistan and Chechnya. You are the ones who brought forth the band of heroes in the New York and Washington conquests [9/11 attacks]...we will not forget the heroism of the Muslim Palestinian woman in the sacred land and her great stands that many men could not equal. She has not spared a husband or a son in her support for the blessed al-Aqsa Mosque. She has even offered and sacrificed herself to join the convoy of martyrs so as to find sustenance in the presence of the Lord, thus ignoring all the world's temptations and attractions.

Osama bin Laden, 14 October 2002.

You [the U.S.] are a nation that exploits women like consumer products or advertising tools, calling upon customers to purchase them. You use women to serve passengers, visitors, and strangers to increase your profit margins. You then rant that you support the liberation of women.

Al Qaeda, 24 November 2002.

We will stand covered in our veils and abayas [robes worn by Saudi women], with our weapons in our hands and our children in our arms.

Al-Khansaa, August 2004.

We love Allah and His Messenger [Muhammad]. We march in a single path, the path of jihad for the sake of Allah, and our goal is martyrdom for the sake of Allah, and our goal is [to gain] the pleasure of Allah and His Paradise...We stand shoulder to shoulder with our men, supporting them, helping them and backing them up. We educate our sons, and we prepare ourselves...The blood of our husbands and the body parts of our children are the sacrifice by means of which we draw closer to Allah.

Al-Khansaa, "Our Goal is Paradise." August 2004.

The female jihad warrior must be familiar with various types of weapons and ammunition, and with how to disassemble, clean, reassemble, use and shoot a weapon... She is a female jihad warrior who wages jihad by means of funding jihad; she wages jihad by means of waiting for her jihad warrior husband and when she educates her children to that which Allah loves.

She wages jihad when she bears arms to defend her family...
She wages jihad when she shows patience and fortitude with
her husband who is waging jihad for the sake of Allah. She
wages jihad when she supports jihad and when she calls for
jihad in word, deed, belief and prayer.

Al-Khansaa, "Obstacles in the Path of the Jihad Warrior
Woman." August 2004.

The striptease campaign still continues, and the so-
called Saudi regime's Channel Two is still presenting women,
[as it has] since it was founded...The women of the Arabian
Peninsula appear on the television screens on the news
programs [as broadcasters]. Moreover, even the correspondents
are sometimes female. Women on news [programs] have today
become a requirement, while in the past there was no need for
it whatsoever.

Al-Khansaa, "The Feminine View." August 2004.

WOMEN AND CHILDREN, THE KILLING
OF

Our religion forbids us to kill innocents—children and
women who are not combatants. Women soldiers who place
themselves in the battle trenches receive the same treatment as
fighting men.

Osama bin Laden, 28 May 1998.

The Islamic movement has the right to sacrifice whoever it sees fit. The rule is that [Muslim] children, women, and the weak should not be a goal except in one situation: if it is difficult to win without sacrificing them.

Sheikh Omar bin Bakri Muhammad, 13 September 1999.

First of all, we must clarify an important issue, and this is whether America is a country of war or a country with which we have an agreement...It is agreed that it is a country of war, and it is permitted for Muslims to strike a country of war with all [kinds] of blows, because the blood, money, and honor of its residents are permitted...the sanctity of the blood of women, children, and the elderly [from a country of war] is not absolute...

...It is permitted for Muslims to kill inviolable infidels [children, women, and the elderly] in order to repay in kind. If the infidels target Muslims women, children, and elderly, then it is permitted for Muslims to repay them in kind and kill [their women, children, and elderly] as they killed...

...It is permitted for Muslims to kill inviolable infidels in the event that they [the Muslims] attack them and cannot differentiate between those with immunity and the warriors or fortifications and, accordingly, they are permitted to kill them as a result [of inability to distinguish] and not with premeditation...

...It is permissible for Muslims to kill inviolable infidels if they are aiding the fighting in deed, word, opinion, or any other way...

...It is permitted for Muslims to kill inviolable infidels when there is a need to burn the fortifications or the fields of the enemy in order to weaken his strength, to breach the ramparts, or to topple the country, even if the inviolable ones die as a result...

...It is permitted for Muslims to kill inviolable infidels if they need to use heavy weapons that cannot differentiate between those who are inviolable and the warriors...

...It is permitted for Muslims to kill inviolable infidels if the enemy uses women and children as a human shield, and it is not possible to kill the warriors except by killing this shield. In such a case it is permitted to kill them all.

...It is permitted for Muslims to kill inviolable infidels if the latter had an agreement with the Muslims and broke the agreement, and the imam had to kill the inviolable ones to make an example of them.

The Crusader Oppressor Salah al-Din, September 2001.

The killing of innocent civilians, as America and some intellectuals claim, is really very strange talk. Who said that our children and civilians are not innocent and that shedding their blood is justified? That it is lesser in degree? When we kill their innocents, the entire world from east to west screams at us, and America rallies its allies, agents, and the sons of its agents. Who said that our blood is not blood, but theirs is? Who made this pronouncement? Who has been getting killed in our countries for decades? More than one million children, more than one million children died in Iraq and others are still dying. Why do we not hear someone screaming or condemning, or even someone's words of consolation or condolence?

Osama bin Laden, 21 October 2001.

However, this prohibition of the killing of children and innocents is not absolute. It is not absolute. There are other texts that restrict it. I agree that the Prophet Muhammad forbade the killing of babies and women. That is true, but this is not absolute. There is a saying, 'If the infidels killed women and children on purpose, we shouldn't shy way from treating them in the same way to stop them from doing it again.' The men that Allah helped [9/11 attacks] did not intend to kill babies; they intended to destroy the strongest military power in the world, to attack the Pentagon that houses more than 64,000 employees, a military center that houses the strength and the military intelligence.

Osama bin Laden, 21 October 2001.

In my view, if an enemy occupies a Muslim territory and uses common people as human shields, then it is permitted to attack that enemy. For instance, if bandits barge into a home and hold a child hostage, then the child's father can attack the bandits and in that attack even the child may get hurt.

Osama bin Laden, 7 November 2001.

There is no doubt that Allah has ordered us to target the unbelievers, to kill them and to fight them, by any means that can achieve this goal, even if [those hurt] by these means include [not just] those infidels against whom war is being waged—who are the intended targets—but also those who are not intended as targets, such as women, children, and other such infidels who intentional killing is not permitted. This is what the Muslim jurists conventionally define as 'collateral killing.' The legitimacy of these [means] has been established even if [their use] result in the killing of a number of Muslims...This is justified under the principle of overriding necessity, due to the fact that it is impossible to avoid and to distinguish between them and those infidels against whom war is being waged and who are the intended targets.

Abu Mus'ab al-Zarqawi, 18 May 2005.

WORLD TRADE CENTER BOMBING (26 FEBRUARY 1993)

I have no connection or relation with this explosion.

Osama bin Laden, March 1997.

Ramzi Yousef [mastermind of the bombing], after the World Trade Center bombing, became a well-known Muslim personality, and all Muslims know him. Unfortunately, I did not know him before the incident. I remember him as a Muslim who defended Islam from American aggression. He took this effort to let the Americans know that their government assaults

Muslims to insure Israeli interests, to insure the Jews. America will see many youths who will follow Ramzi Yousef.

Osama bin Laden, 28 May 1998.

WORLD VIEW

It should not be hidden from you that the people of Islam have suffered from aggression, iniquity and injustice imposed on them by the Zionist-Crusaders' alliance and their collaborators, to the extent that the Muslims' blood became the cheapest and their wealth as loot in the hands of the enemies. Their blood was spilled in Palestine and Iraq. The horrifying pictures of the massacre of Qana, in Lebanon, are still fresh in our memory. Massacres in Tajikistan, Burma, Kashmir, Assam, the Philippines, Fatani [sic —perhaps Thailand's Muslim-dominated Pattani province], Ogaden, Somalia, Eritrea, Chechnya and in Bosnia-Herzegovina took place, massacres that send shivers in the body and shake the conscience. All of this and the world watched and heard, and not only didn't respond to these atrocities, but also with a clear conspiracy between the U.S. and its allies and under the cover of the iniquitous United Nations, the dispossessed people were even prevented from obtaining arms to defend themselves.

Osama bin Laden, 23 August 1996.

What bears no doubt in this fierce Judeo-Christian campaign against the Muslim world, the likes of which has never been seen before, is that the Muslims must prepare all the possible might to repel the enemy in the military, economic, missionary, and all other areas. It is crucial for us to be patient and to cooperate in righteousness and piety, and to raise awareness to the fact that the highest priority, after faith, is to repel the incursive enemy which corrupts the religion [Islam] and the world.

Osama bin Laden, October/November 1996.

The Arabian Peninsula has never...been stormed by any forces like the Crusader armies spreading in it like locusts, consuming its riches and destroying its plantations. All this is happening at a time when nations are attacking Muslims like people fighting over a plate of food.

World Islamic Front for Jihad against the Jews and Crusaders, 23 February 1998.

We indubitably think there is a global heresy, [spread] by the Jews and the Christians—and headed by America, the spearhead of heresy, which genuinely occupies Muslim lands, plunders their resources, exiles their sons, and carries out a series of illegitimate actions in order to gain control and influence. What the Jews are doing in Palestine is decisive proof.

Sulaiman Abu Ghaith, 10 July 2001.

It has become clear to us from past experience that America is a country warring against Islam and Muslims. Indeed, it is its greatest enemy. It uses war against Islam, and crimes and corruption that are inconceivable to humankind. Thus, it should be treated according to the laws of war on Islam, and not according to [laws] of peace.

Abd al-Aziz bin Saleh al-Jarbu', November 2001.

[The alliance of Muslim groups represents] a growing power that is rallying under the banner of jihad for the sake of Allah and operating outside the scope of the New World Order. It is free of the servitude for the dominating Western empire. It promises destruction and ruin for the new Crusades against the lands of Islam. It is ready for revenge against the head of the world's gathering of infidels, the United States, Russia and Israel. It is anxious to seek retribution for the blood of the martyrs, the grief of the mothers, the deprivation of the orphans, the suffering of the detainees, and the scores of the tortured people throughout the land of Islam, from Eastern Turkistan to Andalusia.

Ayman al-Zawahiri, 2 December 2001.

The issues of Al Qaeda are those of the Muslim community in Afghanistan, Somalia, Bosnia and Chechnya. The main motive of these operations is the defense of the Islamic sacred places.

Al Qaeda, 26 April 2002.

We live in an unstable international situation, or more correctly in a transitional period to which the rules applied in normal conditions do not apply. It also does not have the prerequisites to survive for long...The United States, which has become the uncontested sole superpower, is...taking a direct approach to secure its interests in the world without regard to the interest of others, because it considers itself the sole power in the world and the world should adapt to what it wants.

Al Qaeda in Saudi Arabia, 3 September 2003.

The Islamic nation is today in acute conflict with the Crusaders, their collaborators from among the Jews and the apostates. The enemies of the religion have united to fight the Mujahideen by all ways and means—through the military, intelligence, logistics, economics and the media—and there is no stratagem to fight the Mujahideen that they have not employed.

Mu'aadh Mansour, December 2003/January 2004.

YASSER ARAFAT

The Palestinian state and its treacherous government is headed by the vilest of agents ever in history—Yasser Arafat, who will get what he deserves from Allah.

Al Qaeda in Saudi Arabia, 3 September 2003.

The Zionists...were not satisfied with all the treacherous deeds of the Palestinian Authority and with the repression of the Palestinian Mujahideen by Yasser Arafat and his [Palestinian] Authority in the days of the implementation of the Oslo Accords. The Jews were led by the repeated operations to bypass the collaborator [Arafat], and occupy the territories in order to punish the [Palestinian] Mujahideen by themselves.

Louis Attiya Allah, 20 January 2004.

YEMEN

This is a warning to Americans in Yemen, the peninsula of Muhammad, Africa, and Asia. If you do not leave our land, we are announcing to you...slaughter...Your tyranny, your arrogance, your cruelty, and your misguidance have increased...Leave our land and stop supporting the plundering Jews. Return to your countries, otherwise the sword will be between us and you. We want you to leave the land of Yemen and the land of the Prophet [Saudi Arabia]. Otherwise, you will reap death because of [your] stupidity in ignoring our warnings to you.

Abu Shihad al-Qandahari, 1 December 2002.

At present one could say that Al Qaeda does not exist in Yemen as an organization, and that there are only individuals who believe in the ideas of Al Qaeda. [The activities of] the organization [in Yemen] came to an end when Sheikh Abu Ali al-Harithi, commander of the organization in Yemen, was martyred...There are many in Yemen who belong to the organization in terms of their sympathies but do not belong to it on the ideological, organizational, and administrative levels, and they are not enlisted [in the organization]... but we do not have peace with the country [Yemen]...Those who carry out operations are not necessarily Al Qaeda members. People without an organizational connection to Al Qaeda are perfectly capable of carrying out operations.

Nasser Ahmad Nasser al-Bahri, 3 August 2004.

YOUTH

Tell the Muslims everywhere that the vanguards of the warriors who are fighting the enemies of Islam belong to them and the young fighters are their sons. Tell them that the nation is bent on fighting the enemies of Islam. Once again, I have to stress the necessity of focusing on the Americans and the Jews, for they represent the spearhead with which the members of our religion have been slaughtered. Any effort directed against America and the Jews yields positive and direct results—Allah willing. It is far better for anyone to kill a single American soldier than to squander his efforts on other activities.

Osama bin Laden, 28 May 1998.

These were popular reactions by young men who willingly offered their lives, seeking the satisfaction of Almighty Allah. I hold in great esteem and respect these great men because they removed the brand of shame from the forehead of our

Muslim community, whether those who carried out attacks in
Riyadh or those who carried out bombing attacks in al-Khobar
and East Africa and other places. I also view with great esteem
our brother cubs in Palestine who are teaching the Jews lessons
in faith and the pride of the faithful.

Osama bin Laden, 10 June 1999.

They [the apostate rulers] tried, using every means and
seduction, to produce a generation of young men that did
not know anything except what [the rulers] want, did not say
anything except what [the rulers] think about, did not live
except according to the rulers' way, and did not dress except in
the rulers' clothes...The bitter situation the Muslim community
has reached is a result of its divergence from Allah's course and
his religious law for all places and times. That bitter situation
came about as a result of its children's love for the world, their
loathing of death, and their abandonment of jihad.

Al Qaeda, 10 May 2000.

In our activity with youth and in [our] preaching and
direction, we sense that the Muslim youth is extremely
perturbed by the American presence in the Arabian Peninsula
and its unlimited support of the Jews. They are looking for
advice on how to remove the Americans from this land—and
this is clearly shown by the martyrdom operations they carry
out, that doubtless constitute the most tremendous acts of
obedience to Allah.

Sulaiman Abu Ghaith, 10 July 2001.

Muslims are being humiliated, tortured and ruthlessly killed all over the world, and it is time to fight these Satanic forces with the utmost strength and power. Today, the whole of the Muslim community is depending (after Allah) upon the Muslim youth, hoping that they would never let them down.

Osama bin Laden, 9 December 2001.

Al Qaeda youths understand very well that either martyrdom or captivity awaits them in their jihad.

Abd al-Rahman al-Rashid, 13-19 October 2002.

The [combat] training tree planted by the Al Qaeda organization in its training camps in Afghanistan has grown and developed in the hearts of Muslim youth, and it has yielded its fruit throughout the world.

Salim al-Makhi, "Mending the Hearts of the Believers." October/November 2002.

It is upon the Muslim youth all over the world, who symbolize the pillar and hopes of this Muslim community, not to follow the propaganda of the hesitators, scaremongers, atheists and liberals, and those who are blended by the West. Furthermore, they should be careful not to be drawn to side-fights that don't contribute to the attacks against the Head of International Disbelief that is represented in the Crusader-Jewish alliance. Moreover, it is important not to get distracted by [fights with] their tails and agents [Arab regimes], which is exactly what the enemies of jihad desire in order to disperse our efforts. Our goal is clear and our guidelines of our policy are well known, for we don't adopt any action that doesn't contribute in the right direction against the Crusader-Jewish alliance.

Sulaiman Abu Ghaith, 7 December 2002.

[In Afghanistan, post U.S. invasion] We differ completely from our enemy [the U.S.] in the psychological fight. While our enemy depended on creating lies about itself, magnifying its power [by saying that] it will not be defeated and the war will not exceed a week...we were working on bonding everyone with Allah and his relation with Him... Therefore, our program depended on building the Muslim person...In fact, we did not suffer much psychologically for the simple reason that we did not make it mandatory for the youth to join the training camps. We opened our nation's eyes on its issues and as a result, the youth came forward to fight for the dignity of Islam and Muslims, armed with the hope of becoming martyrs.

Saif al-Adel, March 2003.

You [the youth] must do something; you must fight the enemies of Allah, the Crusaders and the Jews, and become a bone in their throats and hearts.

Abu Hajjer, October 2003.

Oh youth of Islam, the Crusaders have deployed their bases throughout the Arabian Peninsula, from which the Prophet ordered us to expel them, saying, 'Expel the polytheists from the Arabian Peninsula' and also 'Two religions will not meet on the Arabian Peninsula [meaning only Islam will prevail].' I address my message to [the sons of] the Muslim community and say to them: I swear by Allah that the Jews and the Christians will not leave the Arabian Peninsula unless by jihad, as the ancients expelled them. Do not denigrate yourselves and do not underestimate your abilities. Grasp your weapon and kill the Jews and the Christians wherever they are to be found. You are the offspring of the companions of the Prophet...who broke the noses of the Jews and the Christians, and stepped with their feet on the kings of Persia and Byzantium.

Hazem al-Kashmiri, 17 October 2003.

O Muslim youths! This is our message to you. If we die or get captured, follow the path and do not betray Allah and the Prophet...We should not wait until U.S., British, French, Jewish, South Korean, Hungarian or Polish forces enter Egypt, the Arabian Peninsula, Yemen and Algeria before we resist... We should start the resistance from now. The interests of the Americans, English, Australian, French, Polish, Norwegian, South Korean and Japanese are everywhere.

Ayman al-Zawahiri, 1 October 2004.

SOURCES

1986, April 20: Abdullah Azzam (d. 1989, Mentor to Osama bin Laden)—*The Last Will of 'Abdullah Yusuf' Azzam*. 20 April 1986.

1987, April 15: Abdullah Azzam (d. 1989, Mentor to Osama bin Laden)—*Join the Caravan*. 15 April 1987.

1988, April: Abdullah Azzam (d. 1989, Mentor to Osama bin Laden)—"Al-Qa'idah al Sulbah." *Al-Jihad* 41 (April 1988). 46.

1993, December 6: Osama bin Laden—Robert Fisk. "Anti-Soviet Warrior Puts His Army on the Road to Peace." *The Independent*, 6 December 1993.

1995, April: Osama bin Laden—"Osama bin Laden v. the U.S.: Edicts and Statements." April 1995.

1995, August 3: Osama bin Laden—"An Open Letter to King Fahd in Response to the Latest Ministerial Changes." 3 August 1995.

1996, July 10: Osama bin Laden—"Interview." *Independent* (London), 10 July 1996.

1996, August 23: Osama bin Laden—"Message from Osama

bin-Muhammad bin-Laden to His Muslim Brothers in the Whole World and Especially in the Arabian Peninsula. Declaration of Jihad against the Americans Occupying the Land of the Two Holy Mosques: Expel the Heretics from the Arabian Peninsula." *Al Quds al-Arabi*, 23 August 1996.

1996, October/November: Osama bin Laden—"Exclusive Interview with Osama Bin Ladin: Of Jihad and Terror, the New Powder Keg in the Middle East." *Nida'ul Islam* 15, October/November 1996.

1996, November 27: Osama bin Laden—Abd al-Bari Atwan. "Interview with Saudi Oppositionist Osama Bin Laden." *Al-Quds al-Arabi*, 27 November 1996.

1996, November: Osama bin Laden—Gwynne Roberts. "Dispatches." Channel 4 Television Network [Great Britain], 20 February 1997.

1996, December 6: Osama bin Laden—Robert Fisk. "Interview." *The Independent*, 6 December 1996.

1997, March: Osama bin Laden—Peter Arnett. "Interview." *CNN*, March 1997.

1997, April-May: Abu-Yasir Rifa'i Ahmad Taha (Leader of Egyptian Islamic Group, Linked to Al Qaeda)—"The Islamic State in Egypt in Approaching." *Nida'ul Islam*, April-May 1997.

1998, February 23: World Islamic Front for Jihad against the Jews and Crusaders—"Declaration of the World Islamic Front for Jihad against the Jews and Crusaders." *Al-Quds Al-Arabi* (London), 23 February 1998. Signed by Sheikh Osama bin Muhammad bin Laden, Ayman al-Zawahiri (Emir of the Jihad Group in Egypt), Abu-Yasir Rifa'i Ahmad Taha (Egyptian Islamic Group), Sheikh Mir Hamzah (Secretary of the Jamait-ul-Ulema-e-Pakistan); and Fazlul Rahman (Emir of the Jihad Movement in Bangladesh)

1998, May 28: Osama bin Laden—"To Terror's Source—John Miller's 1998 Interview with Osama Bin Laden." *ABC News*, 28 May 1998.

1998, August 12: Islamic Army for the Liberation of the Holy Places (Linked to Al Qaeda)—"Communiqué." 12 August 1998.

1998, August 12: World Islamic Front for Jihad against the Jews and Crusaders—"Communiqué." 12 August 1998.

1998, August 24: Osama bin Laden—Statement read to *La Republica* (Italy), 24 August 1998.

1998, October 1: Osama bin Laden—"Statement from Khandahar, Where Bin Laden is Based." *Al-Quds Al-Arabi*, 1 October 1998.

1998, December 22: Osama bin Laden—Rahimullah Yousafsai. "Terror Suspect: An Interview with Osama bin Laden." *ABC News*, 26 September 2001.

1999: Esa al-Hindi—*Army of Madinah in Kashmir.* Maktaba Al Ansaar Publications, 1999.

1999, February: Osama bin Laden—John Miller. "Greetings, America: My Name is Osama Bin Laden. Now That I Have Your Attention." *Esquire* 131, February 1999.

1999, May: Sheikh Omar bin Bakri Muhammad (Al-Muhajirun, Claims to be Spokesman for World Islamic Front for Jihad against the Jews and Crusaders)—"Letter to Osama bin Laden." *Almuhajiroun* (Internet), May 1999.

1999, June 10: Osama bin Laden—Salah Najm. "Osama Bin Laden, the Destruction of the Base." *Al Jazeera*, 10 June 1999.

1999, September 13: Sheikh Omar bin Bakri Muhammad (Al-Muhajirun, Claims to be Spokesman for World Islamic Front for Jihad against the Jews and Crusaders)—*Roz al-Youssef* (Egypt), 13 September 1999.

1999, September 27: Omar ibn al-Khattab (d. 2002, Al Qaeda Commander of Islamic Brigade in Chechnya)—"Interview." Azzam Publications, 27 September 1999.

1999, December 21: Nazeer Ahmed Mujjaid—Fax to Voice of America on 21 December 1999.

2000, January 5: Masood Azhar (Chief of Jaish-e-Muhammad, Linked to Al Qaeda)—"Speech." 5 January 2000.

2000, January 26: Hafiz Muhammad Saeed (Commander of Lashkar-e-Taiba—Linked to Al Qaeda—Pakistan/Kashmir)—"Speech." *Dawacenter* (Internet), 26 January 2000.

2000, May 10: Al Qaeda—"Declaration of Jihad against the

Country's Tyrants, Military Series." Recovered by Manchester, Great Britain, Police on 10 May 2000.

2000, May 30: Sheikh Omar bin Bakri Muhammad (Al-Muhajirun, Claims to be Spokesman for World Islamic Front for Jihad against the Jews and Crusaders)—"Interview." *The Jerusalem Post*, 30 May 2000.

2000, June 22: Osama bin Laden—"Osama Speaks on Hijrah and the Islamic State." *Al-Jihad Newsletter*, no. 4, Supporters of Shariah, (Internet), 22 June 2000.

2000, August 20-27: Osama bin Laden—"Interview (Written) of Osama Bin Laden." *Ghazi Magazine*, 20-27 August 2000.

2000, October 18: Abu-Yasir Rifa'i Ahmad Taha (Leader of Egyptian Islamic Group, Linked to Al Qaeda)—"Communiqué." 18 October 2000.

2000, November 12: Abu-Yasir Rifa'i Ahmad Taha (Leader of Egyptian Islamic Group, Linked to Al Qaeda)—"Communiqué." 12 November 2000.

2001, June 20: Osama bin Laden—*Reuters*, 20 June 2001.

2001, July: Ahmed Ressam (Al Qaeda Operative Who Failed to Bomb Los Angeles Airport in December 1999)—"Testimony." Southern District Court of New York, July 2001.

2001, July 10: Sulaiman Abu Ghaith (Al Qaeda Spokesman)—"Opposite Direction." *Al Jazeera*, 10 July 2001.

2001, September: The Crusader Oppressor Salah al-Din—"The Truth of the New Crusader War." September 2001.

2001, September 16: Fatwa on General Pervez Musharraf and the U.S.A.—The Shari'a Court in Lahore, Pakistan, The London School of Shari'a, The Society of Muslim Lawyers Committee for the Defense of Legitimate Rights, The Khilafah Movement, and The Islamic World League, 16 September 2001.

2001, September 19: Jaish-e-Muhammad, Harkat-ul-Mujahideen, Al Badr and Jamiat-ul-Mujahideen (Linked to Al Qaeda)—Joint Statement, 19 September 2001.

2001, September 21: Mullah Omar (Taliban Leader)—Voice of America. "Interview" (Not Broadcast). *Guardian* (Great Britain), 26 September 2001.

2001, September 24: Osama bin Laden—"Open Letter to Fellow Muslims in Pakistan." *Al Jazeera*, 24 September 2001.

2001, September 27: Abu Hamza (Egyptian Cleric, Supporter of Various Jihad Organizations)—"Interview." *Christian Science Monitor*, 27 September 2001.

2001, September 28: Osama bin Laden—"The United States Should Search within Itself: Exclusive Interview with Osama Bin Laden." *Ummat* (Karachi, Pakistan), 28 September 2001.

2001, September 29: 9/11 Hijackers—"Letter left by 9/11 Hijackers." *Los Angeles Times*, 29 September 2001.

2001, October 7: Osama bin Laden—*Al Jazeera*, 7 October 2001.

2001, October 9: Sulaiman Abu Ghaith (Al Qaeda Spokesman)—*BBC*, 10 October 2001.

2001, October 10: Abd al-Rahman Salim (Al-Muhajirun Spokesman)—*Al-Hayat al-Jadida* (Palestinian Authority), 10 October 2001.

2001, October 13: Sulaiman Abu Ghaith (Al Qaeda Spokesman)—*Al Jazeera*, 13 October 2001.

2001, October 21: Osama bin Laden—Tayseer Allouni. "Interview." *CNN*, 5 February 2002.

2001, November: Abd al-Aziz bin Saleh al-Jarbu' (Saudi Cleric Who Supports Al Qaeda)—"The Basis for the Legitimacy of the Destruction that Occurred in America." *Al-Neda* Internet), November 2001.

2001, November 2: Mullah Omar (Taliban Leader)—"Letter." (Internet), 2 November 2001.

2001, November 3: Osama bin Laden—"The Century's First War: Speech by Osama bin Laden." *Al Jazeera*, 3 November 2001.

2001, November 7: Osama bin Laden—"Interview." *Dawn* (Pakistan) 10 November 2001.

2001, November 9 ca.: Osama bin Laden. "Dinner Party Tape." Released by U.S. Government on 13 December 2001.

2001, November 9: Ayman al-Zawahiri (Egyptian Al Qaeda Leader)—*Al Jazeera*, 9 November 2001.

2001, November 15: Mullah Omar (Taliban Leader)— "Interview." *BBC*, 15 November 2001.

2001, November 30: Mahfouz Walad al-Walid (Senior Al Qaeda Operative—Abu Hafs 'The Mauritanian')—*Al Jazeera*, 30 November 2001.

2001, December: Abu Ayman al-Hilali (Saudi Al Qaeda Writer)—"Bin Laden and the Palestinian Issue." *Aloswa* (Internet), December 2001.

2001, December 2: Ayman Al-Zawahiri (Egyptian Al Qaeda Leader)—Ayman al-Zawahiri. *Knights under the Prophet's Banner—Meditations on the Jihadist Movement*. London: Al-Sharq al-Awsat, 2 December 2001.

2001, December 9: Osama bin Laden—"Message from Usama Bin Ladin to the Youth of the Muslim Ummah." *Markaz al-Dawa* (Internet), 13 December 2001.

2001, December 26: Osama bin Laden—"The Gaunt Tape." *Al Jazeera*, 26 December 2001.

2002: Jack Roche (Australian Involved in Al Qaeda Plot in Australia)—Notes Seized during Raid on His Home in 2002, Perth, Australia District Court, May 2004.

2002, January: Sulaiman Abu Ghaith (Al Qaeda Spokesman)—
Global Islamic Media (Internet), January 2002.

2002, January 28: Sayf al-Ansari (Pro-Al Qaeda Writer)—
"Fight the Friends of Satan." *Al-Ansar* (Internet), 28 January
2002.

2002, January/February: Abu Ubayd al-Qurashi (Al Qaeda
Military Analyst)—"Fourth Generation Wars." *Al-Ansar*, no.
2, January/February 2002.

2002, February 2: Manual of Afghan Jihad—Al Qaeda, 11
vols., Produced before 9/11 Attacks, *Associated Press*, 2 February
2002.

2002, March 15: Abu Ayman al-Hilali (Saudi Al Qaeda
Writer)—*Al-Ansar* (Internet), 15 March 2002.

2002, April: Sheikh Hamed al-Ali (Saudi Cleric Who Supports
Al Qaeda)—"Fatwa." *H-alali* (Internet), April 2002.

2002, April 2: Taliban Military Commander—"Interview."
Taliban-news (Internet), 2 April 2002.

2002, April 12: Mullah Omar (Taliban Leader) *Al-Neda*
(Internet), 12 April 2002.

2002, April 15: Ahmed al-Haznawi (d. 2001, 9/11 Hijacker)—
"The Wills of the New York and Washington Battle Martyrs."
Al Jazeera, 15 April 2002.

2002, April 15: Ayman al-Zawahiri (Egyptian Al Qaeda

Leader)—"The Wills of the New York and Washington Battle Martyrs." *Al Jazeera*, 15 April 2002.

2002, April 24: Al Qaeda—"A Statement from Qa'idat al-Jihad Regarding the Mandates of the Heroes and the Legality of the Operations in New York and Washington." *Al-Neda* (Internet), 24 April 2002.

2002, April 26: Al Qaeda—"Al-Haznawi: Why the Tape [was released[Now." *Al-Neda* (Internet), 26 April 2002.

2002, May: Abu Ayman al-Hilali (Saudi Al Qaeda Writer)—"The Zionist Terrorism and the Ways to Counter It." *Aloswa* (Internet), May 2002.

2002, May 2: Abdul Adheem al-Muhajir (Al Qaeda Field Commander in Afghanistan)—"Interview." *Al-Sharq al-Awsat*, 2 May 2002.

2002, May 14: Sayf al-Ansari (Pro-Al Qaeda Writer)—"So Fight in the Way of God." *Al-Neda* (Internet), 14 May 2002.

2002, May 23: Osama bin Laden—"Exclusive Transcript of Previously Unaired Interview with Usama Bin Laden." *Qoqaz* (Internet), 23 May 2002.

2002, June 12: Sulaiman Abu Ghaith (Al Qaeda Spokesman)—"Why We Fight America." *Al-Neda* (Internet), 12 June 2002.

2002, June 12: *Al-Ansar*—"The U.S. Deception." *Al-Ansar* (Internet), 12 June 2002.

2002, July 9: Abu Laith al-Libi (Al Qaeda Commander)—
"Statement." *Al-Neda* (Internet), 9 July 2002.

2002, August 10: Sayf al-Ansari (Pro-Al Qaeda Writer)—*Al-Ansar* (Internet), 10 August 2002.

2002, August 24: Sayf al-Ansari (Pro-Al Qaeda Writer)—"Allah Will Torment Them by Your Hands." *Al-Ansar* (Internet), 24 August 2002.

2002, September 10: Abdulaziz al-Omari (d. 2001, 9/11 Hijacker)—Video Will, *Al Jazerra*, 10 September 2002.

2002, September 16: Mullah Omar (Taliban Leader)—
"Message." *Al Jazeera*, 16 September 2002.

2002, September 18: Sayf al-Ansari (Pro-Al Qaeda Writer)—
"The Washington and New York Raid." *Jehad* (Internet), 18 September 2002.

2002, September 27: Kahdaffy Janjalani (Commander of Abu Sayyaf Group, Philippines, Linked to Al Qaeda)—"Statement." 27 September 2002.

2002, October 3: Center for Islamic Studies and Research (Al Qaeda Affiliate)—*Al Neda* (Internet), 3 October 2002.

2002, October 6: Osama bin Laden—*Al Jazeera*, 6 October 2002.

2002, October 8: Abu Ubayd al-Qurashi (Al Qaeda Military Analyst)—"The al-Aqsa Intifada: A Fruitful Jihad and Continued Dedication." *Al-Ansar* (Internet), 8 October 2002.

2002, October 13-19: Abd al-Rahman al-Rashid (Al Qaeda Spokesman)—Mahmud Khalil. "Interview with Al Qaeda Spokesman Abd al-Rahman al-Rashid." *Al-Majallah*, 13-19 October 2002.

2002, October 14: Osama bin Laden—*Al Jazeera*, 14 October 2002.

2002, October 26: Osama bin Laden—"Letter from Usama Bin Ladin to the American People." *Waaqiah.com* (Internet), 26 October 2002.

2002, October/November: Salim al-Makhi (Al Qaeda strategist)—"The Master Trap." The Center for Islamic Studies and Research, *Al-Neda* (Internet), October/November 2002.

2002, October/November: Salim al-Makhi (Al Qaeda Strategist)—"Mending the Hearts of the Believers." The Center for Islamic Studies and Research, *Al-Neda* (Internet), October/November 2002.

2002, November 12: Osama bin Laden—*Al Jazeera*, 12 November 2002.

2002, November 19: Al Qaeda—"An Appeal to Our Brother Workers in the Airbases, Airports, Naval Bases, Seaports, and Others." *Alrakiza* (Internet), 19 November 2002.

2002, November 24: Al Qaeda—"Letter to America." *The Observer* (Great Britain), 24 November 2002.

2002, December: Political Bureau of Al Qaeda—"Communiqué

on the 28 November 2002, Mombasa, Kenya Attacks." *Asfalrasas* (Internet), December 2002.

2002, December 1: Abu Shihad al-Qandahari (Moderator of Islamist Web Forum)—"A Warning to All the Enemies of Allah, the Americans, and Their Jewish, Arab, and Foreign Supporters." *Mojahedoon* (Internet), 1 December 2002.

2002, December 4: Abu Banan (Al Qaeda Operative)— Announcement of Establishment of the Islamic Al Qaeda Organization in Palestine, *Al-Mojahedoon* (Internet), 4 December 2002.

2002, December 7: Sulaiman Abu Ghaith (Al Qaeda Spokesman)—*Al Jazeera*, 7 December 2002.

2002, December 10: Abu Ubayd al-Qurashi (Al Qaeda Military Analyst)—"A Lesson in War." *Al-Ansar* (Internet), 10 December 2002.

2002, December 19: Abu Ubayd al-Qurashi (Al Qaeda Military Analyst) —"A Lesson of War." *Al-Ansar* (Internet), 19 December 2002.

2002, December 26: Abu Shihab al-Qandahari (Moderator of Islamist Web Forum)—"The Nuclear War is the Solution for the Destruction of the United States." *Al-Mojahedoon* (Internet), 26 December 2002.

2003, January 19: Osama bin Laden—"Letter." *Asharq al-Aswat* (London), 19 January 2003.

2003, February: Hafiz Muhammad Saeed (Commander of Laskhar-e-Taiba, Linked to Al Qaeda)—Taped Speech, Rawalpindi, Pakistan, February 2003.

2003, February 11: Osama bin Laden—*Al Jazeera*, 11 February 2003.

2003, March: Saif al-Adel (Al Qaeda Leader)—"Message to Our People in Iraq and the Gulf [Region] Specifically, and to Our Islamic Ummah in General: The Islamic Resistance against the American Invasion of Qandahar and Lessons Learned." *In the Shadow of the Lances*, 5th chapter, March 2003.

2003, April 8: Osama bin Laden—*Associated Press*, 8 April 2003.

2003, April 9: Al Qaeda—"The Crusader War in Iraq." *Al-Neda* (Internet), 9 April 2003.

2003, April 17: Abu Ayman al-Hilali (Saudi Al Qaeda Writer)—"The Fall of the Iraqi Regime." *Al-Ansar* (Internet), 17 April 2003.

2003, April 17: Abu Ubayd al-Qurashi (Al Qaeda Military Analyst)—"Why Did Baghdad Fall?" *Al-Ansar* (Internet), 17 April 2003.

2003, April 17: *Al-Ansar*—"Now the War Has Begun." *Al-Ansar* (Internet), 17 April 2003.

2003, April 25: Al Qaeda—*Al-Neda* (Internet), 25 April 2003.

2003, May 21: Ayman al-Zawahiri (Egyptian Al Qaeda Leader)—*Al Jazeera*, 21 May 2003.

2003, May 21: Sheikh Nasser bin Hamed (Saudi Cleric Associated with Al Qaeda)—*Treatise on the Ruling Regarding the Use of Weapons of Mass Destruction against the Infidels.* Global Islamic Media Center, 23 May 2003.

2003, May 25: Abu Muhammad al-Ablaj (Al Qaeda Spokesman)—"Interview." *Al-Majallah* (Internet), 25 May 2003.

2003, July: Osama bin Laden—*Jahra* (Internet), dated immediately after the fall of the Taliban in November 2001.

2003, August 3: Ayman al-Zawahiri (Egyptian Al Qaeda Leader)—*Al Arabiya*, 3 August 2003.

2003, August 21: Bobby Mahmud (Jemaah Islamiyah, Indonesia—Linked to Al Qaeda)—"Declaration." Australia Broadcasting Corporation, 21 August 2003.

2003, September: Salafist Group for Preaching and Combat (Algeria, Linked to Al Qaeda)—"Proclamation." *BBC*, 23 October 2003.

2003, September 3: Al Qaeda in Saudi Arabia—"The Raid of the 11th of Rabi' al al-Awwal—The Eastern Riyadh Operation and Our War on America and Its Agents." *Faroq* (Internet), 3 September 2003.

2003, September 10: Ayman al-Zawahiri (Egyptian Al Qaeda Leader)—*Al Jazeera*, 10 September 2003.

2003, September 10: Saeed al-Ghamdi (d. 2001, 9/11 Hijacker)—Martyrdom Tape, Al Jazeera, 12 September 2003.

2003, September 28: Ayman al-Zawahiri (Egyptian Al Qaeda Leader)—*Al Jazeera*, 28 September 2003.

2003, October: Sulaiman al-Dosari (Al Qaeda Theoretician)— *The Voice of Jihad*, no. 1, October 2003.

2003, October: Sheikh Nasser al-Najdi (Al Qaeda Theoretician)—*The Voice of Jihad*, no. 1, October 2003.

2003, October: Abu Abdallah al-Sa'di (Al Qaeda Theoretician)—"Explosion Is Not the Way to Reform." *The Voice of Jihad*, no. 1 (Internet), October 2003.

2003, October: Sulaiman al-Dosari (Al Qaeda Theoretician)— *The Voice of Jihad*, no. 2, October 2003.

2003, October: Abu Hajjer (Abd al-Aziz bin Issa bin Abd al-Mohsen, Al Qaeda Leader in Saudi Arabia)—*The Voice of Jihad*, no. 2, October 2003.

2003, October 17: Muhammad bin Shazzaf al-Shahri (Al Qaeda Operative in Saudi Arabia)—"The Wills of the Heroes." Shahab Institute for Media Production, Martyrdom Tape of 12 May 2003 Riyadh Operation Squad Commander, 17 October 2003.

2003, October 17: Hazem al-Kashmiri (Al Qaeda Operative in Saudi Arabia)—"The Wills of the Heroes." Shahab Institute for Media Production, Martyrdom Tape of 12 May 2003 Riyadh Operation, 17 October 2003.

2003, October 17: Muhammad bin Abd al-Wahhab al-Maqit (Al Qaeda Operative in Saudi Arabia)—"The Wills of the Heroes." Shahab Institute for Media Production, Martyrdom Tape of 12 May 2003 Riyadh Operation, 17 October 2003.

2003, October 18: Osama bin Laden—*Al Jazeera*, 18 October 2003.

2003, October 27: Saif al-Adel (Al Qaeda Leader)—*Voice of Jihad*, no. 2, 27 October 2003.

2003, November 14: Abu Salma al-Hijazi (Al Qaeda Operative)—"Interview." *The Fortress* (Internet), 14 November 2003.

2003, December: Louis Attiya Allah (Al Qaeda Author)—*The Voice of Jihad*, no. 6, December 2003.

2003, December: Abu Abd al-Rahman al-Turkemani—"The Final Blows in the Decisive Battles Are At Hand." *Global Islamic Media* (Internet), December 2003.

2003, December 5: Al-Haramain Brigades (Saudi Arabia)—"Communiqué." *Globalislamicmedia* (Internet), 5 December 2003.

2003, December 10: Sheikh Yousef al-Ayiri (d. 2003, Al

Qaeda Commander in Saudi Arabia)—"Jihadi Iraq, Hopes and Dangers." Mujahideen Services Center, (Internet), 10 December 2003.

2003, December 19: Ayman al-Zawahiri (Egyptian Al Qaeda Leader)—*Al Jazeera*, 19 December 2003.

2003, December 31: Sheikh Abu Omar al-Sayf (Saudi Al Qaeda Leader in Chechnya)—*Qoqaz* (Internet), December 2003.

2003, December/January 2004: Abu Hajjer (Abd al-Aziz bin Issa bin Abd al-Mohsen, Al Qaeda Leader in Saudi Arabia)— "The Guerrilla War." *Al-Battar*, no. 1, December 2003/January 2004.

2003, December/January 2004: Mu'aadh Mansour (Al Qaeda Military Analyst)—"The Importance of Military Preparedness in Shari'a." *Al-Battar*, no. 1, December 2003/ January 2004.

2003, December/January 2004: Introduction, *Al-Battar*, no. 1, December 2003/January 2004.

2004, January: Al Qaeda—Internal Al Qaeda Training Manual. *UPI*, 13 February 2004.

2004, January 2: The Islamic Army in Iraq—"A Message to the American People." 2 January 2004.

2004, January 4: Osama bin Laden—*Al Jazeera*, 4 January 2004.

2004, January 9: Nabil Sahraoui (d. 2004, Commander of the

Salafist Group for Preaching and Combat in Algeria, Linked to Al Qaeda)—"Interview." *Al-Hayat* (London), 9 January 2004.

2004, January 20: Sheikh Abdallah al-Rashoud (d. 2005, Al Qaeda theologian)—*Voice of Jihad*, no. 9, 20 January 2004.

2004, January 20: Editorial Board—*Voice of Jihad*, no. 9, 20 January 2004.

2004, January 20: Louis Attiya Allah (Al Qaeda Author)—"Commentary on Bin Laden's Speech." *Voice of Jihad*, no. 9, 20 January 2004.

2004, January 20: Abu Abdallah al-Sa'di (Al Qaeda Writer)—"The Experience of Jihad and the Dead End." *Voice of Jihad*, no. 9, 20 January 2004.

2004, February 24: Ayman al-Zawahiri (Egyptian Al Qaeda Leader)—*Al Arabiya*, 24 February 2004.

2004, March 13: Abu Dujan al-Afghani (Military Spokesman for Al Qaeda in Europe)—Claims Responsibility for 11 March, Madrid Bombings, 13 March 2004.

2004, March 29: Abdul Aziz al-Muqrin (d. 2004, Al Qaeda Military Commander in Saudi Arabia)—"The Targets inside the Cities." *Al-Battar*, 29 March 2004.

2004, April 15: Osama bin Laden—*Al Arabiya*, 15 April 2004.

2004, April 16: Brigades of Muhammad Atta (The Base for Jihad)—"Communiqué." 16 August 2004.

2004, April 27: Abdul Aziz al-Muqrin (d. 2004, Al Qaeda Military Commander in Saudi Arabia)—*The Guardian*, 28 April 2004.

2004, May 6: Osama bin Laden—Offers Gold for Assassinations, Various Islamist Websites, 6 May 2004.

2004, May 11: Abu Mus'ab al-Zarqawi (Al Qaeda Leader in Iraq)—"Statement at the Execution of Nicholas Berg." *al-Muntada* (Internet), 11 May 2004.

2004, May 14: Abdul Aziz al-Muqrin (d. 2004, Al Qaeda Military Commander in Saudi Arabia)—"Statement." (Internet), 14 May 2004.

2004, May 17: Shamil Basayev (Chechen Mujahideen Commander)—Claims Responsibility for Assassination of Chechen President Akhmad Kadyrov on 9 May 2004. *Kavkazcenter* (Internet), 17 May 2004.

2004, May 30: Al Quds Company of Al Qaeda in the Arabian Peninsula—Claims Responsibility for 29 May Attack on al-Khobar, 30 May 2004.

2004, June: Fawwaz bin Muhammad al-Nashami (Commander of 29 May 2004 Attack at Khobar, Saudi Arabia)—"Interview." *Voice of Jihad*, June 2004.

2004, June 6: Al Qaeda in the Arabian Peninsula—"Notice in

Regard to Warning the Muslims from the Crusaders and the Heretics." 6 June 2004.

2004, June 11: Ayman al-Zawahiri (Egyptian Al Qaeda Leader)—*Al Arabiya*, 11 June 2004.

2004, June 13: Al Qaeda Organization in the Arabian Peninsula—"The 13th News Report in Regard to the Kidnapping of an American Aviation and Engineer and the Killing of Another." 13 June 2004.

2004, June 19: Al Qaeda Organization in the Arabian Peninsula—"The 14th News Communiqué in Regard to the Execution of the American Prisoner Paul Marshall." 19 June 2004.

2004, June 19: Abdul Aziz al-Muqrin (d. 2004, Al Qaeda Commander in Saudi Arabia)—"The Story of the American POW: Apache Engineer Paul Marshall." *Voice of Jihad*, no. 19, 19 June 2004.

2004, June 20: Jamaat al-Tawhid and Jihad (Iraqi Insurgent Group)—*Al Jazeera*, 20 June 2004.

2004, June/July: Sheik Ubay Abd al-Rahman al-Athari bin Bajad al-'Utaybi (Saudi Cleric)—"Oh Demonic Rulers, There Will Be No Surrender!" *Voice of Jihad*, no. 20, June/July 2004.

2004, July 28: Abu Hafs al-Masri Brigades (Existence is Doubted by Some Experts)—"Communiqué." 28 July 2004.

2004, July 30: Islamic Jihad Movement in Uzbekistan—"Communiqué." 30 July 2004.

2004, August: *Al-Khansaa*—Women's Information Bureau in the Arabian Peninsula, August 2004. Has articles "Our Goal is Paradise"—"Obstacles in the Path of the Jihad Warrior Woman"—and "The Feminine View."

2004, August 3: Nasser Ahmad Nasser al-Bahri (Formerly Osama bin Laden's Bodyguard)—*Al-Quds al-Arabi* (London), 3 August 2004.

2004, August 26: Al-Islambouli Brigades (Chechnya)—"Communiqué." *Islamic-Minbar* (Internet), 26 August 2004.

2004, August 31: Information Council of Kabardino-Balkarian Islamic Jammat (War Council) 'Yarmuk'—Kavkaz Center, 31 August 2004.

2004, August/September: Abd al-Rahman ibn Salem al-Shamari (Al Qaeda Writer)—*Voice of Jihad*, no. 23, August/September 2004.

2004, September: Imam Samudra (Member of Jemaah Islamiyah, Indonesia –Linked to Al Qaeda, Sentenced to Death for Bali Bombing 12 October 2002)—*I Fight Terrorists*. September, 2004.

2004, September 9: Ayman al-Zawahiri (Egyptian Al Qaeda Leader)—*Al Jazeera*, 9 September 2004.

2004, September 9: Jemaah Islamiyah (Indonesia, Linked to Al

Qaeda)—Statement Claiming Responsibility for Car Bombing of Australian Embassy on 9 September 2004. *Enda* (Internet), 10 September 2004.

2004, September 13: Harun Ilhan (Turk, Indicted for Istanbul Bombings 20 November 2003)—Testimony in Turkish Court, *BBC*, 13 September 2004.

2004, September 13: Adnan Ersoz (Turk, Indicted for Istanbul Bombings 20 November 2003)—Testimony in Turkish Court, *BBC*, 13 September 2004.

2004, September 15: Islamic Army of Iraq—"Statement." *Iaminiraq* (Internet), 15 September 2004.

2004, September 17: Shamil Basayev (Chechen Mujahideen Commander)—Claims Beslan School Attack. *Kavkazcenter* (Internet), 17 September 2004.

2004, September 22: Al-Jihad Organization in Iraq—"Communiqué." 22 September 2004.

2004, October: Sa'ud bin Hamoud al-Utaybi (d. 2005, Al Qaeda Leader in Saudi Arabia)—"Editorial." *Voice of Jihad*, no. 27, October 2004.

2004, October: Patani United Liberation Organization (Thailand, Separatist Group)—"Communiqués." *Pulo* (Internet), October 2004.

2004, October: Sheikh Aaamer bin Abdallah al-Aamer (Saudi

Al Qaeda Writer)—"Men of Jihad, This Is Your Festive Season." *Voice of Jihad*, no. 27, October 2004.

2004, October 1: Ayman al-Zawahiri (Egyptian Al Qaeda Leader)—*Al Jazeera*, 1 October 2004.

2004, October 17: Tawhid and Jihad (Iraq, Abu Mus'ab al-Zarqawi's Group)—Media Information Department, 17 October 2004.

2004, October 28: Assam the American (Adam Gadhan—American Member of Al Qaeda)—Al-Sahab Productions, August 2004.

2004, October 29: Osama bin Laden—"Address to the American People." *Al Jazeera*, 29 October 2004.

2004, November 1: Al Qaeda's Committee in the Arabian Peninsula—*Voice of Jihad*, no. 28, 1 November 2004.

2004, November 9: Abu Anas al-Maghribi (Of the Europe and America Branch of Al Qaeda)—*Al-Ma'sada* (Internet), 9 November 2004.

2004, November 10: *Al-Battar* (Al Qaeda Military On-Line Magazine)—*Al-Battar*, no. 2, 10 November 2004.

2004, November 17: Abu Abd al-Rahman al-Athari Sultan ibn Bijad (Pro-Al Qaeda Writer)—"Letter." *Islahi* (Internet), 17 November 2004.

2004, November 19: International Association of Muslim Scholars—"Communiqué." 19 November 2004.

2004, November 29: Ayman al-Zawahiri (Egyptian Al Qaeda Leader)—*Al Jazeera*, 29 November 2004.

2004, December: Sheikh Abu Omar al-Sayf (Mufti of the Jihad Fighters in Chechnya): "Open Letter to the Jihad Warriors in Iraq Regarding Democracy and the Elections." *Al-Faath Magazine*, December 2004.

2004, December 9: The Military Committee of Abu Anas al-Shami Brigade—Al Qaeda Media Committee in Iraq, 9 December 2004.

2004, December 27: Osama bin Laden—"To the Muslims in Iraq in Particular and the [Islamic] Nation in General." Al-Sahab Institute for Media Productions, 27 December 2004.

2004, December 30: Army of the Supporters of the Sunna, The Jihad Warriors Army and the Islamic Army in Iraq—Joint Statement "The Farce of Democracy and Elections." *Al Jazeera*, 30 December 2004.

2005, January 8: Abu Yasser Sayyaf (Media Representative of the Salahst Group for Preaching and Combat—"Communiqué." 8 January 2005.

2005, January 16: Islamic Army in Iraq—"Final Statement to All Who Desire Security." *Al-Ma'sada* (Internet), 16 January 2005.

2005, January 23: Abu Mus'ab al-Zarqawi (Al Qaeda Commander in Iraq)—*Islah* (Internet), 23 January 2005.

2005, January 26: Al Qaeda in Iraq—*Islam-Minbar* (Internet), 26 January 2005.

2005, January 30: Ayman al-Zawahiri (Egyptian Al Qaeda Leader): *Al Jazeera*, 10 February 2005.

2005, January 31: Abu Omar Abdul Bir (Media Wing of Salafist Group for Preaching and Combat—linked to Al Qaeda—Algeria)—"Interview." *Al-Faath Magazine*, 31 January 2005.

2005, February 1: Peninsula Lions Brigades (Kuwait)—"Communiqué." *Alseyassah* (Internet), 1 February 2005.

2005, February 14: Al Qaeda Organization in Greater Syria—Message from Tanzim al-Qaeda fi Bilad al-Sham (Al-Qaeda Organization in the Land of [Greater] Syria). (Internet), 14 February 2005.

2005, February 21: Al Qaeda in Iraq—*Al-Saqifa* (Internet), 21 February 2005.

2005, March 2: Abu Maysara (Media Agent for Abu Mus'ab al-Zarqawi's Group in Iraq)—"This Is Our Identity." *The Pinnacle*, 3 March 2005.

2005, March 2 : Abu Bakr Naji (Al Qaeda Strategist)—*The Management of Barbarism. Al-Ikhlas* (Internet), 2 March, 2005.

2005, March 16: Al Qaeda in Iraq—"Communiqué." Al Qaeda's Jihad Committee in Mesopotamia, 16 March 2005.

2005, April 4: Al Qaeda in Iraq—Al Qaeda Media Committee, 4 April 2005.

2005, April 24: Al Qaeda in Iraq—"Statement from Al Qaeda in Response to Those Who Take Part in the Government of Cross Worshippers and Apostates." 24 April 2005.

2005, April 29: Abu Mus'ab al-Zarqawi (Al Qaeda Commander in Iraq)—"O People of Islam! Strength! Strength!" Al Qaeda's Jihad Committee in Mesopotamia, 29 April 2005.

2005, May: Louis Attiyah Allah (Al Qaeda Author)– "Letter to British Prime Minister Tony Blair." Al Qaeda Media Committee, May 2005.

2005, May 1: Al Qaeda in Iraq—"Communiqué." Al Qaeda's Jihad Committee in Mesopotamia, 1 May 2005.

2005, May 8: Abu Soheib Miliani (Al Qaeda in Algeria)— "Letter." 8 May 2005.

2005, May 10: Al Qaeda in Iraq—"Communiqué." Al Qaeda's Jihad Committee in Mesoporamia, 10 May 2005.

2005, May 11: Abu Abdul Rahman al-Iraqi (Deputy Chief of Al Qaeda in Iraq)—"Statement." Al Qaeda's Jihad Committee in Mesopotamia, 11 May 2005.

2005, May 13: Al Qaeda in Iraq—Media Information Department, 13 May 2005.

2005, May 14: Al Qaeda in Iraq—Al Qaeda Media Committee, 14 May 2005.

2005, May 18: Abu Mus'ab al-Zarqawi (Al Qaeda Commander in Iraq)—"The Return of Ibn Al-'Alqami's Grandchildren." *Alheshah* (Internet), 18, May 2005.

2005, May 21: Hizb ut-Tahrir (Pan-Islamist Organization)— "Communiqué." 27 May 2005.

2005, June 17: Ayman al-Zawahiri (Egyptian Al Qaeda Leader)—*Al Jazeera*, 17 June 2005.

GLOSSARY OF TERMS

Al-Aqsa Mosque: located in Jerusalem

Allah: "God," a contraction of the Arabic *al-il h*, "The God"

Emir: a commander, ruler, prince

Emirate: from the Arabic *imarah*, "right to rule," the rule or jurisdiction of an emir

Fatwa: an Islamic decree or religious pronouncement invoked by a religious authority

Hadith: "Sayings," or "Report," a literary form that communicates a "custom" or "tradition" of the Prophet Muhammad

Jihad: "Striving in God's cause to achieve spiritual excellence"," for militant Muslim fundamentalists used frequently for holy war

Ka'ba: Literally "cube," the main Islamic sanctuary in Mecca

Land of the Two Holy Mosques: Land of *Harramain*—the entire Arabian peninsula

Land of the Two Rivers: Iraq

Mujahid: singular, one who strives for spiritual excellence, also an adjective

Mujahideen: plural of *mujahid*, for militant Muslim fundamentalists means warriors fighting for Islam

The Prophet: Muhammad

Qur'an: "Recitation," the holy scripture of Islam

Shari'a: Islamic religious law based on the Qur'an and Hadith

CHRONOLOGY OF EVENTS

1979, December: Soviet army invades Afghanistan.

1980-1986: Bin Laden helps organize the Muslim resistance in Afghanistan.

1988: Al Qaeda founded in Afghanistan.

1991: U.S. installs its military bases in Saudi Arabia.

1991, April: Bin Laden leaves Saudi Arabia after opposing the kingdom's alliance with the United States. He goes to Afghanistan, then to Khartoum in Sudan, where he stays for five years.

1993, February 26: World Trade Center bombed, killing six and injuring more than 1,000.

1993, October 4: Al Qaeda-trained fighters kill 18 U.S. soldiers in Somalia.

1994-1996: First Chechen War: Chechen separatist forces force Russian troops out of Chechnya.

1995, November 13: Five Americans and two Indians die and 60 injured in truck bombing of a U.S.-operated Saudi National Guard training center, the Khobar Towers.

1996, May: Bin Laden leaves Sudan and returns to Afghanistan.

1996, June 25: Truck bombing of al-Khobar Towers in Dhahran, Saudi Arabia, killing 19 American servicemen and wounding 500.

1996, August 23: Bin Laden's declaration of war against the U.S.

1998, February 23: Declaration of the World Islamic Front for Jihad against the Jews and Crusaders.

1998: August 7: U.S. embassies in Dar es Salaam, Tanzania and Nairobi, Kenya bombed by Al Qaeda, killing 224 people and injuring 5,000.

1998, August 20: U.S. missile attack destroys several training camps in Afghanistan and the Al Sifa pharmaceutical factory in Sudan.

1999-now: Second Chechen war—Russian army returns to Chechnya after Chechen attacks in Moscow and neighboring areas.

1999, December: Plots to attacks tourist sites in Jordan and bomb Los Angeles airport fail.

2000, October 12: Suicide boat attack on USS *Cole* in Yemeni port of Aden kills 17 U.S. sailors, 39 injured.

2000, December 24: Christmas Eve bombings of churches in

Indonesia by Jemaah Islamiyah, kill 22 people and wound nearly 100.

2001, September 11: Two planes hit the World Trade Center, one plane hits the Pentagon, and another crashes in Pennsylvania—2,976 people die.

2001, Dec. 13: Assault on Indian Parliament in New Delhi by Jaish-e-Muhammad and Lashkar e-Toiba organizations.

2002, April 11: Suicide truck bomb explodes near ancient Jewish shrine of El Ghriba on Tunisian island of Djerba, killing 14 Germans, five Tunisians and a Frenchman.

2002, May 8: Suicide bomber kills 11 French navy experts and three Pakistanis outside Sheraton Hotel, Karachi, Pakistan.

2002, October: Theater siege in Moscow, Russia, Chechens take hostages, 129 hostages and 41 Chechens die.

2002, October 6: Explosion rips through French oil tanker Limburg, off the coast of Yemen, killing one crewman.

2002, October 12: Bombs explode in Bali, Indonesia, killing 202 and injuring 132.

2002, November 28: Car bomb at Israeli-owned Paradise Hotel in Mombassa, Kenya, kills 18 and injures 80. Minutes after two missiles narrowly miss Israeli holiday jet on take-off from the city's airport.

2003, March 18: U.S.-led coalition attacks Iraq.

2003, May 1: Bush announces end of major combat operations in Iraq.

2003, May 12: Suicide bombers in vehicles shoot their way into housing compounds for expatriates in Riyadh, Saudi Arabia, killing 35, including 8 Americans, more than 160 wounded.

2003, May 16: Salafia Jihadia sets off at least five explosions in Casablanca, Morocco, which hit a Spanish restaurant, a hotel and a Jewish community center, killing 45 people, including 12 bombers, and wounding about 100.

2003, August 5: Suicide car bombing of Marriott Hotel in Jakarta, Indonesia kills 12 and wounds 150.

2003, August 19: Truck bombing of U.N. headquarters in Baghdad kills 22, including Sergio Vieira de Mello, top U.N. envoy to Iraq.

2003, November 8: Suicide bombing of housing compound in Riyadh, Saudi Arabia kills at least 18 and wounds more than 120.

2003, November 15: Two synagogues in Istanbul, Turkey attacked by suicide bombers, killing 25 and wounding 300.

2003, November 20: Car bomb explodes at the HSBC Bank Headquarters in Istanbul and a second detonates near British consulate, killing 27 and wounding more than 400.

2004, March 11: 191 people die and 1,453 wounded in bomb attacks on trains at Madrid, Spain by Moroccan Islamic Combat Group.

2004, April 15: Osama bin Laden offers Europe a truce—rejected by all countries.

2004, May 9: Chechen President Akhmad Kadyrov assassinated by Chechen jihadists in bomb blast that killed six others and wounded around 60.

2004, May 29: Al Qaeda attacks foreign company compounds in Khobar, Saudi Arabia, killing at least 22 people.

2004, June 18: Paul M. Johnson Jr., American engineer working in Saudi Arabia, kidnapped on 12 June and beheaded by Al Qaeda on 18 June.

2004, June 22: Kim Sun-il beheaded by Jamaat al-Tawhid and Jihad (Iraqi insurgent group) after South Korean government rejected the captors' demands that it halt the scheduled deployment of more troops to Iraq.

2004, August 24: Female suicide bombings of two Russian passenger jets by Chechen militants, killing all 90 passengers and crew.

2004, August 31: At least 10 dead and over 50 injured by female suicide bomber in central Moscow.

2004, September 1-3: Chechen militants hold hostages in school in Beslan, North Ossetia, Russia, results in 326 dead and 727 injured.

2004, September 9: Jemaah Islamiyah bombs Australian Embassy in Jakarta, Indonesia, killing nine and wounding 173.

2004, October 7: Bombing of Egyptian resort at Taba, Egypt kills 36, including 26 Israelis and seven Egyptians, and wounds 105.

2004, December 27: Osama bin Laden recognizes Abu Mus'ab al-Zarqawi as Emir of Al Qaeda operations in Iraq.